Brought to you by

SUPERKID ACADEMY
A SIMPLE GUIDE FOR HOME USE

Easy to Use!

SWEET LIFE
LIVING IN GOD'S BLESSING

BIBLE STUDY FOR KIDS!

Ordinary kids doing extraordinary things through the power of God's Word!

Unless otherwise noted, all scripture is from the *Holy Bible, New Living Translation* © 1996, 2004 by Tyndale Charitable Trust. Used by permission of Tyndale House Publishers.

Scriptures marked AMP are from *The Amplified Bible, Old Testament* © 1965, 1987 by the Zondervan Corporation. *The Amplified New Testament* © 1958, 1987 by The Lockman Foundation. Used by permission.

Scriptures marked KJV are from the *King James Version* of the Bible.

Scriptures marked MSG are from *The Message* © 1993, 1994, 1995, 1996, 2000, 2001, 2002. Used by permission of NavPress Publishing Group.

Scriptures marked NIV are from *The Holy Bible, New International Version* © 1973, 1978, 1984, 2011 by Biblica Inc. Used by permission. All rights reserved worldwide.

Scriptures marked NKJV are from the *New King James Version* © 1982 by Thomas Nelson Inc.

Superkid Academy Home Bible Study for Kids—Sweet Life—Living in God's BLESSING

ISBN 978-1-60463-099-2					30-1066

© 2010 Eagle Mountain International Church Inc. aka Kenneth Copeland Ministries. All rights reserved.
New material added © 2012 Eagle Mountain International Church Inc. aka Kenneth Copeland Ministries. All rights reserved.

Kenneth Copeland Publications
Fort Worth, TX 76192-0001

For more information about Kenneth Copeland Ministries, visit kcm.org or call 1-800-600-7395 (U.S. only) or +1-817-852-6000.

SuperkidAcademy.com • 1-800-606-4190

TABLE OF CONTENTS

WELCOME! v
ACKNOWLEDGMENTS vi
A SIMPLE GUIDE vii
HEALTH & SAFETY DISCLAIMER x
WEEK 1: THE SWEET LIFE 11
WEEK 2: "X" MARKS THE SPOT 27
WEEK 3: STAY ON THE PATH 43
WEEK 4: SELL OUT! 55
WEEK 5: ALL OF MY HEART 69
WEEK 6: ALL OF MY MIND 83
WEEK 7: ALL OF MY BODY 97
WEEK 8: ALL OF MY PAST 111
WEEK 9: ALL OF MY PRESENT 125
WEEK 10: ALL OF MY FUTURE 139
WEEK 11: FAITH 153
WEEK 12: HOPE 165
WEEK 13: LOVE 179

WELCOME!

Dear Parent/Teacher,

Thank you for your purchase of the Superkid Academy Curriculum!

Please use the following URL to access your Bonus Downloads Section:

http://www.superkidacademy.com/downloads

I believe you will experience great and exciting things as you begin the faith adventure of *Superkid Academy Home Bible Study for Kids—Sweet Life—Living in God's BLESSING*.

As you launch into this faith-building time with your family or small group, take the opportunity to seek the Lord's direction about how to minister these lessons for maximum impact. God's Word does not return to Him void, and He will see to it that your children are BLESSED and grow strong in faith as you step out in His Anointing to teach them about Him.

Please keep in mind that we are praying for you. We believe and release our faith for a powerful anointing on you as you teach and impart His wisdom, and that your Superkids are strong in the Lord and mighty for Him.

Remember that we here at Academy Headquarters want to be a resource for you. Make sure you are in our contact base so we can keep in touch. And, let us know how we can better serve you and your Superkids.

We love you and look forward to hearing from you!

Love,

Commander Kellie

Commander Kellie

LEADING YOUR SUPERKID ACADEMY:
A SIMPLE GUIDE FOR HOME USE

We are excited that you have brought Superkid Academy into your living room with the Home Bible Study for Kids! This powerful, Bible-based curriculum will guide your children into building a strong, personal relationship with the Lord and inspire them to live an extraordinary, faith-filled life.

Each of the 13 weeks included in this study provide five days of lessons, including a:

- **Lesson Introduction From Commander Kellie:** As the creator of Superkid Academy with more than 20 years' experience ministering to children, Kellie Copeland has a unique anointing and perspective for reaching children with the uncompromised Word of God. She passes on her wisdom through these timeless segments.
- **Lesson Outline:** Each lesson contains three main points, subpoints and supporting scriptures to empower you to clearly communicate the truth to your children.
- **Memory Verse:** Throughout the week, your kids will have the opportunity to memorize and understand a scripture. More than that, they'll learn how to apply it directly to their lives.
- **Bible Lesson:** Each Bible Lesson reinforces the memory verse and the principle behind it. Discussion questions will help you lead your children through not only comprehending the passage of scripture, but also giving it meaning in their lives.
- **Giving Lesson:** Each week, you will have the opportunity to teach your children about the importance of tithing and giving so they can be "blessed to be a blessing" in the Body of Christ.
- **Game Time:** Reinforces the message and gives families an occasion to celebrate what they've learned in a fun way.
- **Activity Page:** Reinforces the lesson through acrostics, word searches, mazes and other puzzles.
- **Supplements:** Support the memory verse and lesson—two will be provided each week, including:
  o **Object Lesson:** Illustrates the focus of the lesson and provides visual and hands-on elements to the teaching.
  o **Real Deal:** Highlights a historical person, place or event that illustrates the current lesson's theme.
  o **Storybook Theater:** Reinforces the message with creative, read-aloud stories.
  o **Food Fun:** Takes you and your children into the kitchen where you will discuss, illustrate and experience God's truth, using everyday items.
  o **Academy Lab:** Brings the lesson and science together.

And, don't forget the enclosed Praise and Worship CD! These original, upbeat, kid-friendly songs put the Word in your children's minds and hearts. The CD can be listened to around the house or in the car, and the karaoke, sing-along tracks allow your kids to sing their favorite songs.

Making the Curriculum Work for Your Family

Superkid Academy's Home Bible Study for Kids gives you the flexibility to teach your children in a way that works for you. Each week's lesson is divided into five days of teaching. However, we understand that no two families—or their schedules—are the same, so feel free to adjust the lessons to meet your needs. Use all five days of lessons or select only a few to cover each week. Whether you're using the curriculum as part of your home school, as a boost to your family devotions or in a weekly small group, you have the flexibility to make it work for you.

A Home School Bible Curriculum

Superkid Academy's Home Bible Study for Kids is easy to use, flexible and interactive—no dry Bible lessons here! It is ideal for a variety of learning styles. Each of the 13 weeks contains five days of lessons—one Bible Lesson, one Giving Lesson, one Game Time and two other lessons or stories to support the week's message. You may choose to use all five days of lessons or pick and choose the ones that work best for your educational structure. Optional variations for several of the lessons have been included to meet a variety of needs.

Each week's Lesson Outline provides the major points of the lesson and the Snapshot includes a list of supplies needed for that week, allowing you to easily prepare and customize each week's lessons. Here are just a few additional ideas for customizing for your home school:

- Reread the Bible passage each day throughout the week to give your children—and you—time to meditate on the highlighted scripture
- Use one or more of the discussion questions as a journaling exercise
- Begin a weekly, family Game Night
- Use the Storybook Theater in your nighttime read-aloud routine.

Family Devotions

Superkid Academy's Home Bible Study for Kids empowers you to disciple your children and teach them the Word of God in an easy, fun way. You may choose to use all five days' worth of lessons, or select only a few. Each lesson takes less than 15 minutes, so the curriculum fits easily into your busy life.

Lessons are numbered 1–5, giving you the flexibility to include whichever lesson fits your daily schedule for that week. This allows you freedom to plan around work schedules, church commitments and extracurricular activities. Here are two sample schedules:

5-Day Schedule

Sunday—Church (no lesson)

Monday—Bible Lesson

Tuesday—Object Lesson

Wednesday—Mid-week services (no lesson)

Thursday—Giving Lesson

Friday—Storybook Theater

Saturday—Game Time

3-Day Schedule

Sunday—Church (no lesson)

Monday—Bible Lesson

Tuesday—Soccer practice (no lesson)

Wednesday—Giving Lesson

Thursday—Soccer practice (no lesson)

Friday—Object Lesson

Saturday—Family time (no lesson)

A Weekly Small Group

Superkid Academy's Home Bible Study for Kids is designed for use over several days, but a week's worth of lessons can easily be consolidated for a small group. Simply choose the lessons that work best for your location and schedule and allow additional time for discussion and prayer.

Sample Small Group Schedule

6 p.m.	Bible Lesson with discussion time
6:30 p.m.	Giving Lesson
6:45 p.m.	Object Lesson and prayer time
7:15 p.m.	Game Time
7:45 p.m.	Refreshments
8:00 p.m.	Closing

Thank you again for implementing Superkid Academy's Home Bible Study for Kids. We stand with you in faith as you disciple your children in the things that matter to Him. Proverbs 22:6 (KJV) says, "Train up a child in the way he should go: and when he is old, he will not depart from it." At Superkid Academy, we are confident that God will bless your efforts, and that you and your children will see the reality of THE BLESSING in all you do (Numbers 6:24-26).

Love,

Commander Kellie
Commander Kellie

HEALTH & SAFETY DISCLAIMER FOR "SUPERKID ACADEMY CURRICULUM"

Superkid Academy is a ministry of Eagle Mountain International Church, aka Kenneth Copeland Ministries (hereafter "EMIC"). The "Superkid Academy Curriculum" (hereafter "SKA Curriculum") provides age-appropriate teaching material to be used in the religious instruction of children. The SKA Curriculum includes physical activities in which children and leaders may participate. Before engaging in any of the physical activities, participants should be in good physical condition as determined by their health care provider. EMIC is not responsible for injuries resulting from the implementation of activities suggested within the SKA Curriculum. Prior to implementing the SKA Curriculum, carefully review your organization's, family's or small group's safety and health policies, as well as food allergies, and determine whether the SKA Curriculum is appropriate for your organization's, family's or small group's intended use.

By purchasing the SKA Curriculum, I, individually and/or as authorized representative for my organization, hereby agree to release, defend, hold harmless, and covenant not to sue EMIC, its officers, deacons, ministers, directors, employees, volunteers, contractors, staff, affiliates, agents and attorneys (collectively, the "EMIC Parties"), and the property of EMIC for any claim, including claims for negligence and gross negligence of any one or more of the EMIC Parties, arising out of my use or organization's use of and participation in the SKA Curriculum, participation in the suggested activities contained within the SKA Curriculum, or resulting from first-aid treatment or services rendered as a result of or in connection with the activities or participation in the activities.

WEEK 1: THE SWEET LIFE

- **DAY 1:** BIBLE LESSON—THE RICH MAN AND JESUS ▶ PG 14
- **DAY 2:** FOOD FUN—HIDDEN CUPCAKES ▶ PG 16
- **DAY 3:** GIVING LESSON—IT NEVER RUNS OUT! ▶ PG 18
- **DAY 4:** STORYBOOK THEATER—A SLAVE'S RANSOM ▶ PG 19
- **DAY 5:** GAME TIME—DIGGING FOR RAISINS ▶ PG 23
- **BONUS:** ACTIVITY PAGE—TREASURE MAZE ▶ PG 25

Memory Verse: "For I know the plans I have for you," says the Lord. "They are plans for good and not for disaster, to give you a future and a hope." —Jeremiah 29:11

Home Bible Study for Kids • Week 1: THE SWEET LIFE

WEEK 1: SNAPSHOT — THE SWEET LIFE

DAY	TYPE OF LESSON	LESSON TITLE	SUPPLIES
Day 1	Bible Lesson	The Rich Man and Jesus	None
Day 2	Food Fun	Hidden Cupcakes	16 Paper baking cups, Hand mixer, Power cord, Mixing spoons, Measuring cups and spoons, Mixing bowl, 2 Cupcake pans, Large chocolate pieces, Ingredients for cupcakes
Day 3	Giving Lesson	It Never Runs Out!	A large purse, Several packs of individually wrapped bubble gum
Day 4	Storybook Theater	A Slave's Ransom	Whiteboard or chalkboard or easel with paper, Dry-erase markers if using whiteboard, Colored chalks if using a chalkboard, Pencil (art pencils work best) and eraser and colored chalks and black marker and rags (to blend chalks) if using paper, Art smock (to keep your artist's clothes clean), see page 19 for optional costumes and props
Day 5	Game Time	Digging for Raisins	2 Bowls of cooked oatmeal per round (6 bowls if playing 3 rounds), 2 Small plates per round (6 plates if playing 3 rounds), 2 Bibs, 1 Table, 20 Raisins per round (60 raisins if playing 3 rounds), Upbeat music
Bonus	Activity Page	Treasure Maze	1 Copy for each child

Lesson Introduction:

This series of lessons is going to be very effective in getting some important core values across to your Superkids. Knowing about The Sweet Life and making a determination in their hearts to live it can affect Superkids for a lifetime! This is the key to our success as believers (Ecclesiastes 12:13). When we teach our kids that God has an amazing life already planned out for them, we arm them with a strong purpose to obey His instructions and directions. From this time forward, when you can at any time refer to The Sweet Life, your Superkids will think, *God has an awesome plan for me.* You've actually given them a way to understand "THE BLESSING"—that's what The Sweet Life really is.

The other important core value to be grasped has to do with the pirates! This is a great way for the kids to catch the concept of how sin will keep them from walking in THE BLESSING! They'll say, "Don't let that pirate _____ defeat you." They'll fill in the blank (strife, fear, doubt, etc.). They'll catch the concept.

Kids change, families change and churches change when they choose The Sweet Life plan!

Love,

Commander Kellie

Commander Kellie

Series: Sweet Life

Lesson Outline:

You are embarking on an exciting journey with your children this week, one that will affect the rest of their lives. As you begin putting the lessons in this study into practice, your children will learn that God has a good plan for their lives. The enemy would love nothing more than to distract them and get them off course, but if they will stay faithful to the plan God has for them, then they will experience His best: The Sweet Life—a glorious, confident and peaceful life in Christ.

I. GOD HAS A GOOD FUTURE PLANNED OUT FOR YOU Jeremiah 29:11-14

    a. God's plan for your future is like a treasure. We call it The Sweet Life!

    b. God's Word tells us, "Seek for Me in earnest, you'll find Me."

    c. To find any valuable treasure takes determination, and to live The Sweet Life requires a decision.

    d. The Father has laid out every moment of your life in advance. Psalm 139:16

II. THE DEVIL IS A THIEVING PIRATE John 10:10

    a. The "pirate" wants to steal our treasure and destroy our future.

    b. The devil's weapons are like pirates.

    c. Some of his "pirates" are greed, selfishness, fear, doubt, strife, stealing and lying.

    d. Other "pirates" can be anger, sadness, jealousy, fear, hatred and death.

III. DON'T LISTEN TO A PIRATE

    a. The pirate's plan is to steal, kill and destroy.

    b. God hates sin (pirates) because it keeps you from the treasure.

    c. God's plan is an exciting future of health, wealth and adventure—treasure!

    d. The Sweet Life is a most awesome treasure hunt. Ephesians 2:10 AMP

Notes: _____

_____

_____

_____

Home Bible Study for Kids • Week 1: THE SWEET LIFE

DAY 1: BIBLE LESSON — THE RICH MAN AND JESUS

Memory Verse: "For I know the plans I have for you," says the Lord. "They are plans for good and not for disaster, to give you a future and a hope." —Jeremiah 29:11

This week you will set the foundation for this entire study. You will teach your children about the truth of God's love for His people and His good plan for our lives. His only requirement is that we love and obey Him and His Word. Enjoy this special time of opening God's Word with your children and sharing the truth in it.

Read Luke 18:18-23:
The Rich Man

Once a religious leader asked Jesus this question: "Good Teacher, what should I do to inherit eternal life?"

"Why do you call me good?" Jesus asked him. "Only God is truly good. But to answer your question, you know the commandments: 'You must not commit adultery. You must not murder. You must not steal. You must not testify falsely. Honor your father and mother.'"

The man replied, "I've obeyed all these commandments since I was young."

When Jesus heard his answer, he said, "There is still one thing you haven't done. Sell all your possessions and give the money to the poor, and you will have treasure in heaven. Then come, follow me."

But when the man heard this, he became very sad, for he was very rich.

Discussion Questions:

1. **What question did the religious ruler ask Jesus?**
   He asked Jesus how to receive eternal life.

2. **What did he mean by "eternal life"?**
   He wanted to know how to go to heaven and live with God forever.

3. **What was Jesus' first response?**
   Jesus said the man should follow the Ten Commandments.

4. **What was the man's response to this?**
   He said that he had already done that.

5. **What did Jesus tell him to do next?**
   Jesus told him to give all his money to the poor.

6. **What was the man's response?**
   He was very sad.

7. **Was the man's money the real issue that Jesus was trying to point out? If not, then what was the real issue?**
   No, the man's money was not the issue. The real issue was the man's devotion to material things. He loved his money more than he loved Jesus.

Series: Sweet Life

8. **What can we learn from this story?**
   Our love for God should be greater than our love for anything else.

9. **Our memory verse this week, Jeremiah 29:11, says, "'For I know the plans I have for you,' says the Lord. 'They are plans for good and not for disaster, to give you a future and a hope.'" What can we learn from that scripture and how does it apply to this lesson?**
   God wants the best for us, and He has great plans for our future. Whatever He has for us is much better than anything we can do, create or build for ourselves.

Notes: _____
_____
_____
_____
_____
_____
_____
_____
_____
_____
_____
_____
_____
_____
_____
_____
_____
_____
_____
_____
_____
_____
_____
_____

Home Bible Study for Kids • Week 1: THE SWEET LIFE

DAY 2: FOOD FUN — HIDDEN CUPCAKES

Suggested Time: 10 minutes

Memory Verse: "For I know the plans I have for you," says the Lord. "They are plans for good and not for disaster, to give you a future and a hope." —Jeremiah 29:11

Supplies: ☐ 16 Paper baking cups, ☐ Hand mixer, ☐ Power cord, ☐ Mixing spoons, ☐ Measuring cups and spoons, ☐ Mixing bowl, ☐ 2 Cupcake pans, ☐ Large chocolate pieces, ☐ Ingredients for cupcakes

Lesson Instructions:

Who's ready to enjoy something sweet today? I have a great chocolate cupcake recipe. Would you like to help me?

(Talk about how you planned out your "Food Fun" lesson)

- Making your list
- Shopping
- Gathering your supplies
- Preparing everything for your Superkids

You know, this recipe reminds me today about The Sweet Life God has planned out for you. There are no yucky parts in His plan. We just have to follow the recipe for our lives from beginning to end. *(By reading the recipe, you can gain momentum as you describe all the sweet things in the recipe and how delicious they are when combined together.)*

(Have the children combine all the ingredients and pour half the batter in the paper baking cups.)

In this recipe today, we are holding back half the mix because we want to put something really yummy in the center of this batter.

Can anyone guess what the ingredient is?

That's right: the chocolate! Chocolate is so good when it melts in your mouth, and that is exactly what is going to happen on the inside of these cupcakes.

(Make an indentation in each cupcake. Have your children put the individual pieces of chocolate in the center of each one, and pour the remaining batter on top.)

Thanks for your help, today. It looks like we are all done.

(Act surprised when you put the cupcake pan in your oven and realize you forgot to preheat it.)

(Very dramatic) OH NO! I promised you we were going to enjoy something sweet today, didn't I? Let me start from the beginning and go over each step *(realizing you didn't write down preheating the oven)*.

What am I going to do?

This reminds me about Jeremiah 29:11. I am so glad God doesn't say "OH NO!" when it comes to our lives. His plans for you are so big that He already planned out The Sweet Life for you to enjoy! *(At this time, preheat the oven and then bake the cupcakes.)*

Series: Sweet Life

Home Bible Study for Kids • Week 1: THE SWEET LIFE

This would have been a disaster if we hadn't discovered our mistake. I am so thankful! And just like we enjoy the sweet surprises our Father plans for us, you can enjoy a bite of The Sweet Life that was planned for you, today! *(Once the cupcakes are finished baking, allow the children to enjoy them.)*

Notes: _____

Home Bible Study for Kids • Week 1: THE SWEET LIFE

DAY 3: GIVING LESSON — IT NEVER RUNS OUT!

Suggested Time: 10 minutes

Offering Scripture: And the homes of the upright—how blessed! Their houses brim with wealth and a generosity that never runs dry. —Psalm 112:2-3 MSG

Supplies: ☐ A large purse, ☐ Several packs of individually wrapped bubble gum (placed inside the purse)

Lesson Instructions:

Hey, kids! Check out this big purse! Today, I want to tell you a story about a big, old purse just like this one.

There was once a sweet, old great-grandma who had a huge purse just like this one! Her name was Annie. How do I know this grandma was sweet? Well, she loved Jesus with all her heart, and she was always talking to her family about how wonderful God is. This grandma had lots and lots of grandkids and great-grandkids. They all loved Grandma Annie's big purses because… *(Begin digging in the large purse and pull out a piece of gum.)* they knew every time they saw her, they'd get a piece of bubble gum from her huge purse. And even though Grandma Annie had lots and lots of grandkids, never once did she not have enough bubble gum for every one of them. That purse must have been pretty heavy just from all the gum inside!

There is a scripture in Psalms that describes this grandma pretty well. It says, "And the homes of the upright—how blessed! Their houses brim with wealth and a generosity that never runs dry."

Don't you think this scripture describes Grandma Annie? The Word teaches us that upright people who love God and obey Him will be blessed. It also teaches us that the upright will have plenty to give AND they'll have generous hearts. Perhaps the most important part of this scripture says their giving will never run dry—just like Grandma Annie's purse that never runs out of bubble gum!

What can you do to be like Grandma Annie? Just have a generous heart and love God. Be ready to give at any moment. When you do that, God will do His part and make sure you always have plenty to bless others with. Your supply will never run out!

Notes: _____
_____
_____
_____
_____
_____
_____

Series: Sweet Life

Home Bible Study for Kids • Week 1: THE SWEET LIFE

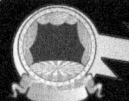

DAY 4: STORYBOOK THEATER — A SLAVE'S RANSOM

Teacher Tip: This segment has many possible variations. Choose the one that best fits your family, and have fun!

List of Characters/Optional Costumes/Props:
- Michael: Cabin-boy hat (red and white cap, or a bandana)
- Joshua: Tattered hat, wig, chains
- Captain Tyrus: Captain's hat, eye patch
- Deven: Silk shirt, gold, clip-on, hoop earring
- Parrot "Firebrand": Beak

Supplies: ☐ Whiteboard, chalkboard or easel with paper, ☐ Dry-erase markers if using whiteboard, colored chalks if using a chalkboard, or pencil (art pencils work best) and eraser and black marker and rags (to blend chalks) if using paper, ☐ Art smock (to keep your artist's clothes clean)

Variation No. 1:

Read the story as part of your read-aloud time.

Variation No. 2:

Read the story as an old-time radio skit, complete with different actors for each part. If you are limited on participants, then have more than one part per person and change the voice. Make copies of the skit and have each actor highlight his or her lines.

Variation No. 3:

Act out the story as a fun skit. Perhaps your children can practice during the day (even creating fun costumes from everyday items), and then perform in the evening for the whole family. Before beginning your skit, remember to introduce your cast!

Variation No. 4:

Create a storybook theater where one or more family members sketch the story on a whiteboard, chalkboard or artist's easel, as another member reads the story. Initially, there will be a few supplies to purchase, but don't let this be a deterrent from using the illustrated story option! Once the supplies have been purchased, they'll be long-lasting and reusable. Teacher tip: If using an easel, cut the paper to fit on the board and tape it down. Lightly sketch the drawing with a pencil prior to presentation. Time may not allow for the picture to be completely drawn and colored during the story. Erase the pencil lines, so light lines are visible to you but not to your audience. Review the story ahead of time to determine the amount of time needed to complete the illustration. When the story begins, use black marker to draw the picture, following the sketched pencil lines. Next, apply color using the colored chalks. Then, blend the color with the rags. Finally, cut the illustration from the board, roll it up, secure with rubber bands, and share it with one of the kids!

Home Bible Study for Kids • Week 1: THE SWEET LIFE

Story:

Young Michael had been a slave of the ferocious pirate ship *Infernus* all of his days—about 12 years. But nobody was counting, for he was but a lowly cabin boy. He whistled as he swabbed the lowest deck of the ship. It was the one job that gave him comfort of late. His only friend in the world was a prisoner in one of the cells he took extra care in mopping. It was curious to think that Michael did not even know the name of his best friend. No one had ever shown him the kindness that this young man showed toward Michael. As Michael worked, his friend joined in to whistle a tune until the captain hollered from above, as he usually did.

"Orphan!" The captain's growl pierced the air.

"I gotta go," Michael whispered to his friend.

"Orphan! Where is that scrawny brat?" The shout came again.

"Why do you let him treat you like that?" asked the prisoner. Michael's face paled white in fear as the captain suddenly appeared at the door. Captain Tyrus was the picture of ultimate cruelty, with his hook nose and a sneer that never went away. His one good eye was blacker than sin. And, though short in stature, his appearance was gruesome enough to bring any One-Eyed Jack to his knees.

Captain Tyrus grabbed Michael by the collar. "Where ya been, boy?"

"I been swabbin' the deck, sir...," Michael replied, barely able to speak.

"Ya been swabbin' your gums with the prisoner! Now get back to work or I'll throw ye to the sharks." The captain threw Michael backward and went back up on deck. With his head pounding, Michael picked himself up off the floor.

"Tyrus is awful," the kind prisoner said. "We've got to get out of here."

"That'll never happen. I'm in a stronger prison than you are," Michael retorted in defeat.

"There is a way. But you'd have to trust me..."

"I dunno." Escape had never even occurred to Michael.

"Come on, Michael, what have you got to lose?"

"I don't even know your name, and you want to talk mutiny?" Michael began to worry about the unexpected rebel.

"Shhh...just trust me...and I'll trust you."

"Huh?" Michael answered, confused.

"I know I can trust you, Michael, but you have to follow my instructions."

"All right." Michael agreed, realizing he really didn't have anything to lose.

"My name is Josh," the prisoner began. "My father sent me on a quest to bring home some treasure. He gave me a map, but my ship was attacked, and Captain Tyrus stole the map. But, he doesn't know how to use it. We're nearing the island now, and you can take back the map and the treasure. I'll tell you where the map is and how to use it if you promise to return for me."

"Buried treasure? I just wanted to get out of here alive!" Michael exclaimed.

"Well you'll do more than that. We'll split that treasure 50-50. Deal?"

"You bet." Michael and Josh shook hands between the prison cells as they quietly conspired to secure the map's return.

Series: Sweet Life

The next day, Michael could tell that Josh's treasure island was within rowing distance. That night he stole in to the captain's desk and retrieved the treasure map. Then he reported back to Josh as planned. "Now," Josh said, "the captain doesn't know that he's missing the key to the map."

"Which is?"

"My pet parrot...you have to tell him the clues on the map and he'll tell you what they really mean. Kind of like an interpreter. His name is Firebrand. Just call for him, and he'll come to you. But most important: Firebrand doesn't know you, so, you need to give him my name so he'll talk to you."

Suddenly, a thought dawned on Michael. "So that's why you haven't told anyone your name."

"Exactly. And here, take my compass," Josh said, removing the compass from his pocket to Michael's hand.

"Don't worry. I'll return it as quickly as possible."

"I know. Now hurry, before they catch you!"

With lantern, compass and map in hand, Michael tiptoed out of the prison and sneaked into one of the longboats. The night was so black he could barely see the boat slip. But he lowered the boat into the black sea and began his row to freedom. Even in the darkness of the night, he felt lighter and freer than at any time in his life.

As he reached the beach, he was so overcome with joy to be away from the *Infernus,* he wanted to shout and run in his newborn freedom. But he knew that his future freedom still hung delicately. So, the moment he hopped onto the shore, he went straight to work. He called for Firebrand a few times, and it didn't take long for the red and yellow cockatoo to come flapping in. The bird mounted on the boy's shoulder with a loud squawk.

"Shh...," Michael quieted the bird, still fearful of any pirate company.

"Eat more bananas," the parrot said loudly.

"Quiet now...," Michael whispered.

"Eat more bananas," Firebrand interrupted him.

"Shh... no more banana talk. We have got to hurry or the pirates will..."

"Eat more bananas," the parrot interrupted him again.

"Is that all you can say—Eat more..."

"Bananas!" Firebrand finished.

Michael had gotten so caught up in finding the treasure he had forgotten Josh's instruction. "I know," Michael remembered with a start. "Josh—he sent me to talk to you."

"First clue?" Firebrand squawked.

Michael read off the first clue and together the two began to follow the map to a "T." As Michael read off the clues, the parrot interpreted their meaning and led him to each new point. Every so often a booby trap threatened their safety, but Firebrand always knew the best way to dodge them. The two worked long into the night, until neither could go any farther. They fell asleep beside a large palm tree, planning to begin again at first light.

The next morning, there was no small stir among the pirates of the *Infernus.* Just as the sun was rising, a loud, angry growl resounded from below deck, "WHO STOLE MY TREASURE MAP?!"

Infuriated, the captain bounded onto the top deck, shattering anything in his way. He bellowed angry threats to every pirate aboard: "Every knave to the poop deck or be shark's bait!"

Home Bible Study for Kids • Week 1: THE SWEET LIFE

As the crew hit the deck, it didn't take long to discover who was missing. "ORPHAN!" Tyrus called in a rage. Tyrus unsheathed his cutlass as both sword and voice sliced the air, "Return me map, Orphan, or be cut in two!"

The crew spread out to search for Michael until a pirate shouted, "Thar be a longboat missin'."

"Set sail for the island. Make haste, ye blackguards!" the captain barked as he returned to his cabin, followed by his crafty first mate, Deven.

Captain Tyrus never took a liking to being followed by the sound of Deven's peg leg. In his addled state, Tyrus was looking for something to shoot. The moment his cabin door creaked shut, he aimed his pistol at Deven's good leg.

"Wait!" Deven shouted, with hands in the air. "Ye been a-lookin' at the boy's stealin' yer map the wrong way."

"What ye mean?" Tyrus questioned, lowering the pistol.

"I been a-watchin' that orphan boy makin' friends with yer prisoner and methinks he discovered how to decode yer map."

"And how the blazes is that goin' to help us?" Tyrus retorted, throwing his dagger, narrowly missing Deven's skull.

Deven gulped at the knife's nearness and finished his plan. "If the boy knows how to find the treasure, we don't have to. We find the boy, we find the treasure."

"Har, that be a better plan then getting it meself."

TO BE CONTINUED NEXT WEEK…

Original story written by Lyndsey Rae

Notes: _____

_____
_____
_____
_____
_____
_____
_____
_____
_____
_____
_____
_____
_____

Series: Sweet Life

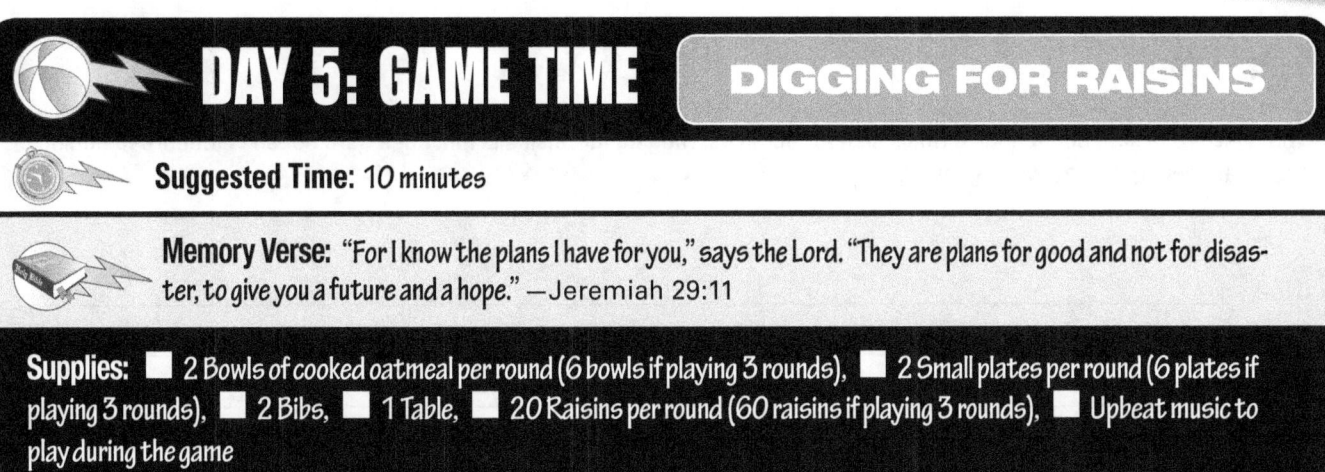

DAY 5: GAME TIME — DIGGING FOR RAISINS

Suggested Time: 10 minutes

Memory Verse: "For I know the plans I have for you," says the Lord. "They are plans for good and not for disaster, to give you a future and a hope." —Jeremiah 29:11

Supplies: ☐ 2 Bowls of cooked oatmeal per round (6 bowls if playing 3 rounds), ☐ 2 Small plates per round (6 plates if playing 3 rounds), ☐ 2 Bibs, ☐ 1 Table, ☐ 20 Raisins per round (60 raisins if playing 3 rounds), ☐ Upbeat music to play during the game

Prior to Game:

Create two teams.

Place two bowls of premade oatmeal on the table.

Place raisins and bibs on the table.

Next to each bowl of oatmeal, place a small plate.

Two players will compete against each other.

Each volunteer will wear a bib.

Set a predetermined amount of time for each "Raisin Round" to be played.

Game Instructions:

Two players will be challenging each other in a raisin-finding contest. Each player will wear a bib because he/she will be finding the raisins, using only his/her mouth. Each player places his/her hands behind his/her back as he/she searches for the raisins.

Tell players, "Let's count together as we place 10 raisins in each bowl of oatmeal." *(Stir the raisins into the oatmeal for an added challenge.)*

When the music starts, each player begins searching for raisins, using only his/her mouth. Once a player has "dug up" a raisin, he/she will transfer it to the plate, using his/her mouth to spit the raisin on the plate. Players should not spit oatmeal onto the plate, only raisins.

Game Goal:

Stop the game when one player finds all 10 raisins, or at the predetermined time. The player with the most raisins on his/her plate wins! If a tie occurs, the player with the least amount of oatmeal on his/her plate wins. If time allows, play additional rounds with new bowls of oatmeal and raisins.

 Home Bible Study for Kids • Week 1: THE SWEET LIFE

Final Word:

Today, we're talking about finding God's plan for our lives. Digging for raisins is fun, but it sure doesn't compare to finding the treasures Jesus has waiting for us.

Notes: _____

_____
_____
_____
_____
_____
_____
_____
_____
_____
_____
_____
_____
_____
_____
_____
_____
_____
_____
_____
_____
_____
_____
_____

Series: Sweet Life

ACTIVITY PAGE — TREASURE MAZE

Memory Verse: "For I know the plans I have for you," says the Lord. "They are plans for good and not for disaster, to give you a future and a hope." —Jeremiah 29:11

The life God has planned for you is truly a treasure. But there is only one path that leads to it. When you follow His map, the Word, you can have The Sweet Life He has for you. Have fun finding the treasure in this maze! (Hint: Only one way leads to the treasure!)

Notes: _____

WEEK 2: "X" MARKS THE SPOT

- **DAY 1: BIBLE LESSON—TREASURE MAP** ▸ PG 30
- **DAY 2: OBJECT LESSON—STUDY YOUR MAP** ▸ PG 32
- **DAY 3: GIVING LESSON—TAKE A LOOK** ▸ PG 34
- **DAY 4: STORYBOOK THEATER—A SLAVE'S RANSOM (PART 2)** ▸ PG 35
- **DAY 5: GAME TIME—TAKE AIM AT THE TREASURE** ▸ PG 39
- **BONUS: ACTIVITY PAGE—TREASURE ACROSTIC POEM** ▸ PG 41

Memory Verse: In him lie hidden all the treasures of wisdom and knowledge. —Colossians 2:3

Home Bible Study for Kids • Week 2: "X" MARKS THE SPOT

WEEK 2: SNAPSHOT — "X" MARKS THE SPOT

DAY	TYPE OF LESSON	LESSON TITLE	SUPPLIES
Day 1	Bible Lesson	Treasure Map	None
Day 2	Object Lesson	Study Your Map	1 Piece of parchment paper (see lesson for alternatives), Magnifying glass, Treasure (ex: a small toy, a pen and notebook/journal, markers, etc.)
Day 3	Giving Lesson	Take a Look	A sack lunch (ex: a sandwich, a piece of fruit or vegetable and a dessert)
Day 4	Storybook Theater	A Slave's Ransom (Part 2)	Whiteboard or chalkboard or easel with paper, Dry-erase markers if using whiteboard, Colored chalks if using a chalkboard, Pencil (art pencils work best) and eraser and colored chalks and black marker and rags (to blend chalks) if using paper, Art smock (to keep your artist's clothes clean), see page 35 for optional costumes and props
Day 5	Game Time	Take Aim at the Treasure	10 Round plastic gold-colored coins, 2 2-Liter bottles (with the word "TREASURE" written down the side), 2 Sheets of construction paper, 1 Felt-tip marker, Masking tape, 1 Card table, 2 Small water bottles labeled "GOD'S WORD," 2 Small squirt guns, Upbeat music
Bonus	Activity Page	Treasure Acrostic Poem	1 Copy for each child

Lesson Introduction:

You are anointed as a Superkid parent to help your children to see God's plan for them as a true treasure to be valued above all other things. When viewed from this perspective, it becomes easy to want to do more than just obey God. It makes us want to fully submit to His will and plan.

Encourage your Superkids to ask God to correct and keep them following His map for their lives. Show them that correction is wonderful. They should look for it whether it comes from parents, teachers, pastors, etc. It's a good thing! And, if they take heed to it, it will help them live a long life (Ephesians 6:1-3).

One day, I asked my father to tell my children the key to finding their destiny. Expecting a lengthy, profound answer, I grabbed my notepad to capture this great lesson. Although wonderfully profound, it wasn't complicated at all. He said, "Well, obey today and at the end of the day, you'll be right where He wants you. Obey tomorrow, the next day and the next, and do that all week—you'll be right where He wants you at the end of the week. Do that for a month, a year, five years, 10 years, a lifetime. You will be and do all that He has called you to be and do!"

Wow! What extraordinary lives our Superkids will lead as they lay hold of this great treasure!

Love,
Commander Kellie

Lesson Outline:

This week, your children will continue to learn about The Sweet Life in Christ that awaits them. Part of walking in that life requires trusting in, turning to and valuing God's Word. So many of the answers your children will need are in the Book. They don't have to wonder and stumble around in the world looking for truth and answers. Their heavenly Father has already provided them. Now, that's good news!

I. GOD'S WORD IS OUR TREASURE MAP Psalm 119:9-13

  a. God has a treasure map that leads to His plan for you. Don't wait!

  b. His Word will lead us to the exact spot where the treasure is.

  c. His map (the Word) will "dig up" our destiny, which is hidden inside our hearts. Ecclesiastes 3:11, AMP

II. FOLLOW THE MAP, FIND THE TREASURE

  a. Following this map takes some searching. Matthew 7:7

  b. If you found a natural treasure map, would you study and follow it?

  c. Studying God's Word closely will help you know which paths to take to find the treasure! James 1:25

  d. You have to value the treasure to want to follow the map.

III. DON'T TRY TO MAKE YOUR OWN MAP James 1:13-17

  a. God has a perfect plan for you to find your treasure. Isaiah 45:2

  b. Don't argue with the Mapmaker. He knows where you need to go. Isaiah 45:11-13

  c. If you follow your own map, you get further away from the treasure "spot." 1 Peter 2:8b: "They stumble because they do not obey God's Word."

  d. Our Father is the ultimate Mapmaker and treasure giver. 1 Corinthians 2:9-12

Notes: _____
_____
_____
_____

Home Bible Study for Kids • Week 2: "X" MARKS THE SPOT

DAY 1: BIBLE LESSON — TREASURE MAP

Memory Verse: In Him lie hidden all the treasures of wisdom and knowledge. —Colossians 2:3

This week, your children will be reminded of the power of God's Word. It is not just a good book, it is <u>the</u> Book. It contains wisdom by which they can—and should—live their lives. Every decision Superkids make, every challenge they face, can be affected by the truth contained within it. That's powerful!

Today, you will be sharing a portion of Psalm 119. This song, which was originally written as a Hebrew acrostic poem, speaks to the truth and power contained in God's Word.

Read Psalm 119: 9-16:

How can a young person stay pure?

By obeying your word.

I have tried hard to find you—

don't let me wander from your commands.

I have hidden your word in my heart,

that I might not sin against you.

I praise you, O Lord;

teach me your decrees.

I have recited aloud

all the regulations you have given us.

I have rejoiced in your laws

as much as in riches.

I will study your commandments

and reflect on your ways.

I will delight in your decrees

and not forget your word.

Discussion Questions:

1. How does this psalm say that a young person can stay pure?
   A young person can stay pure by obeying God's Word.

Series: Sweet Life

2. **What does it mean to "hide God's Word in my heart"?**
   Answers will vary but "to hide God's Word in my heart" can mean that one reads it, meditates on it, honors what it says and even memorizes it. You must make it a priority in your life.

3. **How has the author of this Psalm made God's Word a priority?**
   He has recited it and rejoiced in it as much as in any "thing."

4. **What does the author promise to do in the future?**
   He promises to study God's Word, reflect on it, delight in (or enjoy) it and not forget it.

Variation No. 1: Memorize and Recite

Consider having your children memorize this passage (or the entire Psalm) and recite it for the family at the end of the week.

Variation No. 2: Hebrew Poetry

Psalm 119 is a beautiful example of Hebrew poetry. Older students may benefit from exploring the qualities, structure and purpose of Hebrew poetry as well as giving examples from Scripture. They can share what they learn in a number of ways: a written paper or an oral presentation. This week's activity sheet will give them an opportunity to practice creating an acrostic poem of their own.

Notes: _____

_____
_____
_____
_____
_____
_____
_____
_____
_____
_____
_____
_____
_____
_____

Home Bible Study for Kids • Week 2: "X" MARKS THE SPOT

DAY 2: OBJECT LESSON — STUDY YOUR MAP

 **Suggested Time:** 10 minutes

 **Memory Verse:** In him lie hidden all the treasures of wisdom and knowledge. —Colossians 2:3

 **Teacher Tip:** The goal of this lesson is to demonstrate the difference between glancing at God's Word and really studying it. To find treasure involves a search. God's Word is like that. A proper, thorough search will reveal treasure!

Supplies: ☐ 1 Piece of parchment paper to make a treasure map (can be purchased at office supply stores or you can substitute a piece of brown paper grocery bag or baking parchment, available inexpensively in most large grocery stores), ☐ Magnifying glass, ☐ Treasure (ex: a small toy, a pen and notebook/journal, markers, etc.)

Prior to Lesson:

Hide the "treasure" prior to the lesson. Create a treasure map by wrinkling a piece of parchment paper. Draw a simple picture of the room, home or yard; include pictures of objects located in the area. The map can have written clues or pictures drawn on it to help locate the treasure.

Lesson Instructions:

You may not realize it, but there is a treasure hidden in this room (or home or yard). It's true, right here in our home there is a treasure! Now, we could all start looking for it, but it may be a lot easier to use a map.

Do you have a map?

(Look at each child, as if searching for one with a map.)

No?

Well, the good news is I have a map that will show us exactly where to find our hidden treasure!

Can you help me read this map? If we can find the treasure, it is ours to keep!

(Choose someone who can read or follow the drawings on the map. Allow him or her to glance at the map for only a moment, then roll it back up.)

All right, let's find the hidden treasure!

(It will be challenging to locate the treasure with only a glance at the map.)

Why aren't you finding the treasure?

(Let children explain they need to see the map a little longer.)

Do you think it will help to keep the map with you?

Series: Sweet Life

Home Bible Study for Kids • Week 2: "X" MARKS THE SPOT

(Allow children to take the map on the treasure hunt. When the treasure is located, offer them the treasure as a reward for a diligent search. This is a perfect illustration to explain to your children that God's Word is our treasure map. Be sure to emphasize the difference between a glance and a search. When our heavenly treasure map is with us, we find the treasure every time!)

Final Word:

Remember Colossians 2:3 says that "in him lie hidden all the treasures of wisdom and knowledge." So don't go anywhere without the most awesome treasure map ever made. God has given it to us because He wants us to find His treasure!

Notes: _____
_____
_____
_____
_____
_____
_____
_____
_____
_____
_____
_____
_____
_____
_____
_____
_____
_____
_____
_____
_____
_____
_____

Series: Sweet Life

Home Bible Study for Kids • Week 2: "X" MARKS THE SPOT

DAY 3: GIVING LESSON — TAKE A LOOK

Suggested Time: 10 minutes

Offering Scripture: ...keep your eyes open and be quick to respond. —Romans 12:8 MSG

Supplies: ☐ A sack lunch (ex: a sandwich, a piece of fruit or vegetable and a dessert)

Lesson Instructions:

Today, I have something you are familiar with: a sack lunch.

Let's check out what's inside our bag. *(Remove contents from the bag and place them on a table.)*

Do these things look like they would make a good offering to the Lord?

Well, you wouldn't normally put a sandwich in the offering basket, but I want to tell you a story about a little boy who turned his sack lunches into offerings.

Tyler was in the first grade, and he took a sack lunch to school every day. He enjoyed the cookies his mom packed, so she wasn't surprised when he asked for four instead of two in his lunch one morning. Tyler's mom informed him that two cookies were just right for his sack lunch.

The next day Tyler asked his mom if he could have an extra banana in his sack lunch. His mother let him know that his lunches were plenty big for a boy his size. But on the third day, when Tyler asked for a second sandwich in his lunch, Tyler's mom decided it was time to investigate.

After asking a few questions, she discovered that Tyler had become friends with a boy in his class named Avery who never brought a sack lunch to school. She found out that Tyler had been sharing his lunches with Avery! Well, after learning about the situation, Tyler's mom began packing double lunches, so her son could share his lunch with his new friend.

What a great story! A first-grader, with a generous heart, could use his lunch to bless a classmate who was doing without. Romans 12:8 says, "Keep your eyes open and be quick to respond." Are you ready to be on the lookout for those who need something you have to give? And, don't forget to be quick to respond. If a first-grader can do it, we all can do it!

Notes: _____
_____
_____
_____
_____
_____
_____

Series: Sweet Life

Home Bible Study for Kids • Week 2: "X" MARKS THE SPOT

DAY 4: STORYBOOK THEATER — A SLAVE'S RANSOM (PART 2)

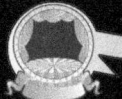

Teacher Tip: This segment has many possible variations. Choose the one that best fits your family, and have fun!

List of Characters/Optional Costumes/Props:
- Michael: Cabin-boy hat (red and white cap, or a bandana)
- Joshua: Tattered hat, wig, chains
- Captain Tyrus: Captain's hat, eye patch
- Deven: Silk shirt, gold, clip-on, hoop earring
- King: Crown
- Parrot "Firebrand": Beak

Supplies: ☐ Whiteboard, chalkboard or easel with paper, ☐ Dry-erase markers if using whiteboard, colored chalks if using a chalkboard, or pencil (art pencils work best) and eraser and black marker and rags (to blend chalks) if using paper, ☐ Art smock (to keep your artist's clothes clean)

Variation No. 1:

Read the story as part of your read-aloud time.

Variation No. 2:

Read the story like an old-time radio skit, complete with different actors for each part. If you're limited on participants, then assign more than one part per person and have them change the voices for each character. Make copies of the skit, and have each actor highlight his or her lines.

Variation No. 3:

Act out the story as a fun skit. Perhaps your children can practice during the day (even creating fun costumes from everyday items) and then perform the skit in the evening for the whole family. Before beginning your skit, remember to introduce your cast!

Variation No. 4:

Create a storybook theater where one or more family members sketches the story on a whiteboard, chalkboard or artist's easel as another member reads the story. Initially, there will be a few supplies to purchase but don't let this be a deterrent from using the illustrated story option! Once the supplies have been purchased, they'll be long-lasting and reusable.

See Week 1 for instructions.

Series: Sweet Life

Home Bible Study for Kids • Week 2: "X" MARKS THE SPOT

Story:

CONTINUED FROM LAST WEEK…

Story Summary:

An orphan boy named Michael is a slave on the pirate ship *Infernus*. Michael becomes friends with Joshua, a prisoner on the ship, taken captive when his own ship was attacked by the *Infernus'* Captain Tyrus, while Joshua was on a quest for buried treasure.

With Joshua's guidance and support, Michael retrieves the stolen treasure map from Captain Tyrus, sneaks off the ship during the night, and rows toward an island in search of the hidden treasure.

Joshua's pet parrot, Firebrand, helps Michael decode the treasure map and avoid booby traps as they search for the treasure. But there's one danger Firebrand can't help Michael with…the pirates of *Infernus,* who are in hot pursuit of Michael and the hidden treasure.

Let's continue…

The two pirates broke out in devious smiles at their plan to catch Michael and the treasure with one blow. The captain added with a sinister snarl, "And when we finds 'em…that orphan's gonna wish he'd never been born!"

Meanwhile, on the island, Michael and Firebrand had set out at dawn to finish the trail to the treasure. The booby traps were becoming more and more difficult to avoid and the clues harder and harder to decipher. But as always, Firebrand somehow knew how to dodge each trap and interpret every clue. Later in the afternoon, the two treasure hunters had come to the very last clue on the map. Firebrand interpreted, "Second and third rock from the cave!"

Michael whispered to Firebrand, "Any hidden traps here?"

From atop his shoulder, Firebrand cawed, "Nets. Walk on leaves." So, carefully Michael stepped over to the rock. When he lifted the second rock, he found a long rope. Under the third rock he discovered a hole just large enough for him to jump through. Then, through the hole was a 15-foot drop…to the greatest treasure Michael had ever seen! Michael gasped as he took in what lay before him. As far as his eye could see, were gleaming mounds of gold, glittering diamonds and every precious stone known to man. His heart skipped a beat at the thought of owning such riches.

Sometime later, as Michael stuck his head up out of the hole, he heard the unmistakable sound of whispers in the trees around him. He turned slowly, knowing the pirates had to be very close by. Reluctantly, Michael realized he had to face them, now. Better to confront them before they reached the treasure! More importantly, he still held two advantages over them: Firebrand's knowledge and the map. But how could he use them to trap the pirates?

Seeing no other way out, Michael summoned up all his courage and shouted, "Captain Tyrus, I know you're out there!"

Caught in his plot, the captain was startled, but he knew how to handle the boy.

"All right, Orphan," he said, as he and his men stepped out from behind the trees, "hand over me map and the bird, and I'll let ye live."

The pirates erupted with laughter until Michael shouted, "It won't do you any good! You don't know how to use it."

"Awww, calm down, me hearty," Tyrus reasoned. "I were just jokin' with ya. Ya know thar be enough loot for all of us. So, I say we go dig up the treasure together."

Remembering Josh, Michael asked, "Where's the prisoner from the ship?"

Home Bible Study for Kids • Week 2: "X" MARKS THE SPOT

"Oh, don't worry yerself about that, me boy. He's safe, and I'll make a bargain with ye: Lead me to the treasure, and ye can both have yer freedom. Ye can be part of our crew, and I'll even give ye a captain's share of the treasure."

This bargain was beginning to sound sweeter and sweeter to Michael. It meant sure freedom for him and Josh. He would even become as rich as the captain. The only problem was that he knew Josh wouldn't approve. Josh would never agree to be part of the *Infernus'* crew. He also knew that Captain Tyrus wasn't one to be trusted in *any* dealings. But, to reject the bargain, he would have to risk everything.

"If you want the treasure map, Tyrus, come and get it!" Michael shouted, decisively.

"So, we have a bargain, eh?" Tyrus grunted as he lowered his gleaming cutlass.

"No," replied Michael. "I'll *never* help fill your treasury or be a part of your crew. If you want this map, you'll have to pry it out of my hands."

The captain was furious. "We have other ways to persuade, ye, Orphan." Shouting angrily at the other pirates, "Well, don't just stand around here, ye bilge rats! Capture him! And remember, if ye damage the map, yer all shark bait! Bring me the map, unharmed!"

Pirate battle cries filled the island as the whole crew ran at Michael.

Fear rose up in Michael, but he tried to keep calm as he watched the men coming closer and closer and heard their fierce cries grow louder and louder. But, as he turned his gaze toward Firebrand, the only thing Michael felt was independence. For the first time in his life, he had stood up to Captain Tyrus. Michael knew Josh would be so proud that he had made the right decision. He closed his eyes, ready to face the crew's punishment. But it never came. Shocked, he opened his eyes to find there were no pirates in sight. But, he could still hear them.

Michael looked up, and to his surprise, the whole pirate crew was trapped in the nets Firebrand had warned him of! Overwhelmed with relief, he suddenly remembered the treasure. But, looking at the nets again, he wondered how long the old trap would hold the whole crew of terrorizing pirates.

"Not long," he said aloud, voicing his own thoughts. Surely, not long enough to carry all the treasure back to the boat and free Josh. There was no question in Michael's mind. He had to go back to the ship without the treasure—and fast, too.

Michael put behind him the dreams of great riches and broke into a sprint, remembering his best friend in the world. He reached the longboat and rowed faster than ever. Upon reaching the ship, he rushed below deck to rescue Josh from his chains. As he began to turn the prison key, Michael apologized, "I don't have the treasure. The pirates caught me, and there was no time to get it and get away from them, too."

But not surprising to Michael, Josh wasn't upset at all. He simply said, "Well then, let's set sail."

"By ourselves?" Michael squeaked, as they reached the top deck.

"Don't worry, I'll steer. Set the sails."

As the wind filled the great, billowing sails and the ship began to slowly gain speed through the choppy, coastal waters, Josh and Michael saw the ship's pirate crew running frantically to the beach. Muffled by the stiff ocean wind, they could faintly hear the captain's raging shriek, "Ye'll never get the boat out of these waters, ya yellow-bellied driftwood. I'll hunt ye down no matter where ye go." The captain's continuing curses were finally drowned out completely as the distance widened and the ship raced into open waters. They were free!

After a few days, Michael began to realize he didn't recognize the waters they now sailed through. He went to his new captain, Joshua, and asked plainly, "Where are we going?"

"Home, of course!" Josh replied.

Series: Sweet Life

Home Bible Study for Kids • Week 2: "X" MARKS THE SPOT

"Where would that be? I've never had a home before," Michael was embarrassed to admit.

"I thought about that, and I know exactly how to fix it. You can live in my house with me."

"Are you sure?" Michael asked in earnest.

"Definitely! I'm sure my parents will love you." Josh's reply almost brought Michael to tears. His life had taken such a dramatic turn. The vision of sailing to a real home gave him a new strength. Michael and Josh doubled their efforts and both sailed with a renewed passion to get home.

After some days, when the crew of two arrived at Josh's home city, Michael was amazed at the welcome they received. There was a huge parade and celebration in the streets. Shouts of joy echoed for miles around as every villager came out to greet the young men. Rolling through the narrow streets lined with jubilant villagers, accompanied by the cheerful sound of the horses' harness bells and the steady clip-clop of hooves, the boys' carriage finally came to a stop, as Josh exclaimed, "We're home!"

Michael's eyes widened in astonishment as he gazed upward, realizing his new home was a great castle. He was tempted to faint as he saw a king, complete with crown and beautiful, royal robes, walking toward *him,* Michael, the lowly slave of a pirate ship.

"Father!" Joshua shouted, as he ran toward the king. Michael could never have imagined this was the kind of home Josh had spoken of. He turned away, not wanting to impose. When Josh said he could live with him, he must have meant as a servant.

As Michael walked away, he heard the king's commanding, yet kind voice, "Where are you going?"

Michael turned, stunned and speechless.

"You can't just walk away from your new family, son."

Michael stammered, "Uh, uh, oh n-no, sir. I-I can be a servant. I don't mind."

But, the king interrupted him, "Joshua did not bring you back here to be a servant. He brought you here to be a prince of the land, an heir of the throne, and to be my son."

Again, Michael was stunned. But, true to the king's word, only a few days later Michael was crowned as the king's own son. He was so caught up in his new life, he completely forgot the treasure. It was a few weeks before Michael recalled the treasure he had lost.

"Father," he hesitantly said, still feeling a bit shy addressing the king in such a familiar way. "Please forgive me for losing the treasure. It was all my fault."

"Come with me," replied the king, as he took Michael and Josh through numerous halls and rooms. Leading them through many secret passageways and hidden halls, the king finally stopped before a beautifully ornate set of double doors. The king took out a large set of golden keys and unlocked the huge doors, saying, "Son, never worry about those small treasures anymore. I have more than enough here, and everything I have is yours."

When the king firmly pushed open the doors, Michael saw masses of fine gold and priceless stones, gleaming in the soft light. Then, his father, with a warm hug for the new prince, added, "Josh brought back all the treasure I was looking for."

THE END

Original story written by Lyndsey Rae

Series: Sweet Life

Home Bible Study for Kids • Week 2: "X" MARKS THE SPOT

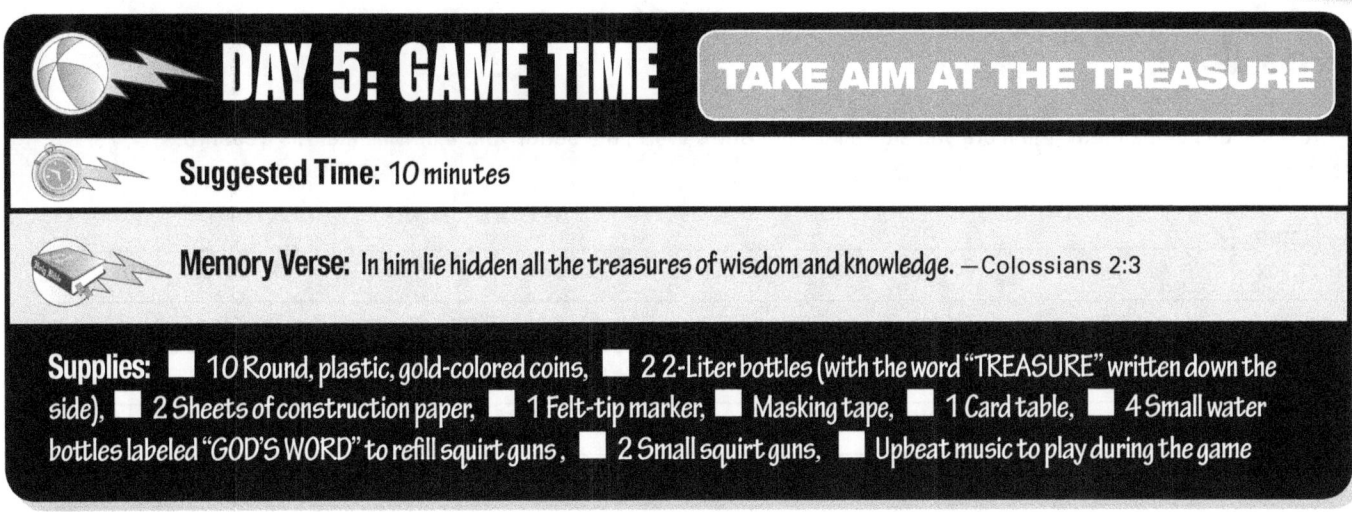

DAY 5: GAME TIME — TAKE AIM AT THE TREASURE

Suggested Time: 10 minutes

Memory Verse: In him lie hidden all the treasures of wisdom and knowledge. —Colossians 2:3

Supplies: ☐ 10 Round, plastic, gold-colored coins, ☐ 2 2-Liter bottles (with the word "TREASURE" written down the side), ☐ 2 Sheets of construction paper, ☐ 1 Felt-tip marker, ☐ Masking tape, ☐ 1 Card table, ☐ 4 Small water bottles labeled "GOD'S WORD" to refill squirt guns, ☐ 2 Small squirt guns, ☐ Upbeat music to play during the game

Prior to Game:

Choose an outdoor area in which to play the game.

Remove the lid from each 2-liter bottle and place the bottles on the table.

Wrap a sheet of construction paper around each 2-liter bottle and, with the felt-tip marker, write the word "TREASURE" down the side of each bottle.

With the marker, write "GOD'S WORD" on each of 2 small water bottles. Balance a gold coin on top each upright 2-liter bottle.

Create a "throw" line, using masking tape, for the players to stand behind.

Play upbeat music during each round of the game.

Game Instructions:

Split into 2 teams.

Each player will get a turn with 1 full squirt gun.

Make a big deal of filling each gun with God's Word.

The object of the game is to knock the gold coins off the bottle tops with 1 full squirt gun.

Once a gold piece or coin is knocked off the bottle, replace it with another, and continue the game.

Game Goal:

The team that knocks the most treasure pieces off the bottles wins.

Series: Sweet Life

 **Home Bible Study for Kids • Week 2: "X" MARKS THE SPOT**

Final Word:

Just like this game today, the more you stay filled with God's Word, the better your aim will be at His treasure!

Notes: _____
_____
_____
_____
_____
_____
_____
_____
_____
_____
_____
_____
_____
_____
_____
_____
_____
_____
_____
_____
_____
_____
_____
_____

Home Bible Study for Kids • Week 2: "X" MARKS THE SPOT

ACTIVITY PAGE — TREASURE ACROSTIC POEM

Memory Verse: In him lie hidden all the treasures of wisdom and knowledge. —Colossians 2:3

This week, you studied Psalm 119, a Hebrew acrostic poem. In this Psalm, the first letter of each stanza, or series of lines that create one section of the poem, begins with one of the 22 letters of the Hebrew alphabet. Today, you get the chance to practice your own acrostic poetry writing skills!

Write a poem about what God's Word means to you, using the letters in the word "TREASURE." Begin each of your sections with the letters below. You may write one line per letter or a stanza with more than one line.

Variation: Dictation

Younger children may need help with this activity. Parents, you may need to coach them as well as allowing them to dictate their poems to you.

TREASURE ACROSTIC POEM

T _____
R _____
E _____
A _____
S _____
U _____
R _____
E _____

Series: Sweet Life

Home Bible Study for Kids • Week 2: "X" MARKS THE SPOT

Notes:

WEEK 3: STAY ON THE PATH

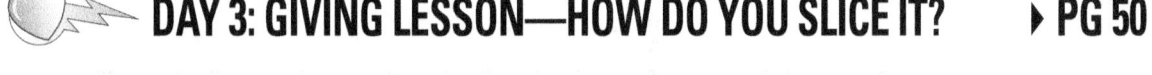 DAY 1: BIBLE LESSON—CHOOSING GOD'S PATH ▶ PG 46

 DAY 2: READ-ALOUD—MAP KEEPERS—
WHO NEEDS A FLASHLIGHT? ▶ PG 48

DAY 3: GIVING LESSON—HOW DO YOU SLICE IT? ▶ PG 50

 DAY 4: OBJECT LESSON—KEEP YOUR TREASURE ▶ PG 51

DAY 5: GAME TIME—NOODLE SEARCH ▶ PG 53

 BONUS: ACTIVITY PAGE—TREASURE HUNT ▶ PG 54

 **Memory Verse:** Your word is a lamp to guide my feet and a light for my path. —Psalm 119:105

Home Bible Study for Kids • Week 3: STAY ON THE PATH

WEEK 3: SNAPSHOT — STAY ON THE PATH

DAY	TYPE OF LESSON	LESSON TITLE	SUPPLIES
Day 1	Bible Lesson	Choosing God's Path	None
Day 2	Read-Aloud	Map Keepers—Who Needs a Flashlight?	None
Day 3	Giving Lesson	How Do You Slice It?	A pie, Small plates, Knife, Forks
Day 4	Object Lesson	Keep Your Treasure	A plastic water bottle, Pliers (or a drill), A small nail, Water (consider adding color to the water), A large bowl
Day 5	Game Time	Noodle Search	1 Case of "ramen" style noodles, 1 Large clear bowl per player, 100 Pennies, Blindfolds, Plates, A large spoon, Upbeat music
Bonus	Activity Page	Treasure Hunt	1 Copy for each child

Lesson Introduction:

For the rest of their lives, our children will have to decide between what God says is true and what a circumstance or fear says to the contrary. Now is the time for them to make a firm choice for all time that God's way is *always* the right way. Their first choice is to put God's Word first place in their hearts, and listen only to that. Second, they must decide once and for all, to *obey* the Word, no matter what comes up or what they think about it.

Psalm 32:8-9 says, "The Lord says, 'I will guide you along the best pathway for your life. I will advise you and watch over you. Do not be like a senseless horse or mule that needs a bit and bridle to keep it under control.'" Lead your children to choose to not allow pirates of any kind to be in charge of their lives! They can decide today to allow the Lord to lead them, trusting His love for them to take them in an awesome direction, giving Him full rein (like the horse) in their lives. No pirate and no circumstance can move them off the path to their treasure!

Love,
Commander Kellie

Series: Sweet Life

Lesson Outline:

There is a very real enemy who would love to distract your children from the plans God has for them. That enemy will lie, steal, cheat and even kill to accomplish his mission. This week, you will teach your children how to avoid his traps. You'll teach them to stand strong on the Word of God so they can avoid the heartache the enemy brings. When they do, they'll be ready to walk in all that God has for them. They'll be ready for The Sweet Life.

I. FOLLOWING GOD'S PATHWAY: THE CHOICE IS YOURS Psalm 77:16-20

    a. Moses chose to follow God's path, even though things didn't look good.

    b. Where was He taking them—toward their treasure or to die in the Red Sea?

    c. God had a plan! Instead of stopping them, the sea stopped the enemy! Isaiah 43:16

    d. God can make a path where there is no path and lead you to your treasure if you follow Him.

II. A PIRATE'S WAY IS DARK; DON'T GO THERE

    a. Pirates try to talk us into leaving God's pathway to our treasure. Some kids leave God's pathway because of distractions.

    b. Sin and disobedience bring darkness! 1 John 1:6

    c. It's hard to see where to go when you are surrounded by darkness. Proverbs 4:19

    d. Never listen to the devil's lying pirates! Ephesians 4:27

III. READING YOUR BIBLE AND LISTENING TO GOD LIGHTS YOUR PATH

    a. The more you put God's Word in your heart, the more light shines on your path. Psalm 119:11, 35, 105

    b. When you are full of light, it's hard for pirates to talk to you. Satan can't figure you out! John 1:5 NKJV

    c. Your treasure, pathway and lamp have been prepared for a long time! Ephesians 2:10

Notes: _____
_____
_____
_____

Home Bible Study for Kids • Week 3: STAY ON THE PATH

DAY 1: BIBLE LESSON — CHOOSING GOD'S PATH

Memory Verse: Your word is a lamp to guide my feet and a light for my path. —Psalm 119:105

Each person makes the choice to either follow God or not. In this week's Bible Lesson, your children will be reminded of a time when another person in history had to make that same choice: Moses. The enemy was hard on his heels, determined to enslave God's people once again. Moses had to make the decision to trust God and lead the people—more than 600,000 men and their families—out of Egypt. The situation looked dim, but God was faithful. He miraculously opened the Red Sea, allowing His people to be saved and stopping the enemy.

God has a plan for His people—even today. And just as He saved the Israelites when it looked as if there was no way out, He will save your children too, if they will choose to follow Him.

Read Psalm 77:16-20:

When the Red Sea saw you, O God,

its waters looked and trembled!

The sea quaked to its very depths.

The clouds poured down rain;

the thunder rumbled in the sky.

Your arrows of lightning flashed.

Your thunder roared from the whirlwind;

the lightning lit up the world!

The earth trembled and shook.

Your road led through the sea,

your pathway through the mighty waters—

a pathway no one knew was there!

You led your people along that road like a flock of sheep,

with Moses and Aaron as their shepherds.

Discussion Questions:

1. **To what period of time in the Bible is this passage of Scripture referring?**
   This passage is referring to Moses leading the Israelites out of Egypt.

Series: Sweet Life

2. **Did Moses know that God would open the Red Sea when he led the people toward it?**
   No, he only followed what the Lord told him to do, step by step.

3. **How do you think Moses and the Israelites felt as they came to the edge of the Red Sea?**
   They were probably scared because they could see the Egyptians coming behind them.

4. **How do you think they felt when they saw the sea part?**
   Allow for all reasonable responses. They were probably relieved and amazed.

5. **What can we learn from this occurrence?**
   We can trust God in all situations, and we should listen to Him every step of the way, knowing that He will make a path, even when there doesn't seem to be one.

Variation No. 1: Personal Experience

Parents, share a time when God made a way out of a difficult situation when there appeared to be none. Talk about when you had opportunities to be distracted by others or the enemy. Share how you came to make a quality decision to follow the Lord and the outcome of it.

Variation No. 2: Journaling

Older children may enjoy journaling about a time when God helped them (or your family) out of a difficult situation. Recording God's goodness and power serves as a powerful reminder for the future. Children will be able to look back at what the Lord has done and say, "God was faithful to me then, and He'll be faithful to me now!"

Notes: _____
_____
_____
_____
_____
_____
_____
_____
_____
_____
_____
_____
_____
_____
_____
_____

Home Bible Study for Kids • Week 3: STAY ON THE PATH

DAY 2: READ-ALOUD — MAP KEEPERS—WHO NEEDS A FLASHLIGHT?

Suggested Time: 15 minutes

Memory Verse: Your word is a lamp to guide my feet and a light for my path. —Psalm 119:105

Story:

Good friends Blake and Alicia stood examining the treasure map. "OK, we know there's a treasure out there," Blake said, "and I think we have all the supplies we need to find it, except a flashlight."

Just then, the sinister and invisible Captain Diablo slid into the room, crept up behind Alicia and whispered in her ear. Though Alicia couldn't see him, she heard his dark whispers and, without realizing it, became his puppet. "A flashlight?" she protested. "I can't carry a dirty, old flashlight. Besides, when you're as bright and beautiful as I am, you don't need any more light!"

Blake shot her a look of dismay before turning back to the map. "Fine, don't carry the flashlight. Just get one, and I'll carry it."

Alicia left to find a flashlight and Blake continued, "Anyway, the most important thing we need to help us find the treasure is this map."

This time, the invisible Captain Diablo moved to whisper in Blake's ear. "Hmmm, I wonder if I should trust this map," Blake said quickly, his confidence wavering. "What if it's fake? It could be wrong. Maybe we're crazy to put our trust in some old map."

Alicia returned with a flashlight and handed it to Blake. Her face reflected just how disgusting she thought the flashlight truly was. "That's not what you said earlier. Remember? You said the map would lead us to the treasure and keep us out of danger."

Blake shook his head, surprised at his own confusion. "You're right. I don't know what I was thinking. I guess I let my feelings get the best of me," he reasoned. "Let's do this! You read the map, and I'll hold the flashlight."

Frustrated, Captain Diablo turned his attention to Alicia and began whispering to her again. Hearing his negative message, Alicia's annoyance grew. "You know I'm terrible at figuring out maps and riddles and stuff," she said testily. "I can't read the map!"

"Well, I can't read the map *and* hold the flashlight," Blake reasoned before turning his attention back to the map. "Dirty or not, you're going to have to hold the flashlight."

Alicia scowled. "Carry a flashlight," she grumbled to herself. "That's just silly. It's not even dark. I just got a manicure. And look, I've already chipped a nail! I'd better go back and get my fingernail file." Alicia put down the flashlight and left to retrieve her manicure set.

Blake continued studying the map, never even noticing Alicia's absence. "I figured it out! OK, all we need to do is head southeast until we see the water tower. Then, we'll go through a tunnel. Good thing we have a flashlight."

At the sight of their confusion, Captain Diablo began dancing. He was sure he had won!

Blake finally looked up and realized that Alicia was missing. "Alicia? Alicia!" he called. "Where in the world did she go? Doesn't she know it's dangerous to go off the path? I hope she's OK. What if something's happened to her?"

Series: Sweet Life

Home Bible Study for Kids • Week 3: STAY ON THE PATH

"This is terrible! Or even worse, what if she's…" He stopped midsentence and finally realized the truth of their situation. "What am I saying?!" he asked in shock. "Shut up, Devil! You're a liar. God gives His angels orders to protect us. I believe Alicia is all right."

Though he couldn't see the effects of his statement, Blake's words hit Captain Diablo like a punch. The villain fell to the ground, choking and gasping for air. Finally, he crawled away.

Blake closed his eyes and began to pray. "Lord, Your Word says that our steps are directed by You. And Your Word is a light to our path. So, Lord, I ask You to help Alicia find her way back. In Jesus' Name. Amen."

As soon as his prayer was finished, Blake opened his eyes and heard Alicia running, barefoot, toward him. She was out of breath, her hair a mess, and her face and hands covered with mud. "Blake, I'm so glad I found you!" she gasped. "I'm sorry I wandered off. I don't know what came over me. Instead of staying focused on our path, I got distracted by my broken fingernail. And NOW, look at me! A broken fingernail is the least of my concerns. Talk about silly!"

"What happened out there?"

"Well, it got so dark I couldn't see, and I ended up in some kind of swamp," she said wild-eyed.

"Where are your shoes?" Blake asked, bewildered.

"I'm not sure," Alicia said, trying to make sense out of her situation. "I didn't freak out until I felt something slimy crawling in my shoe. Then, I really lost it. Too bad, because I really liked those shoes. Apparently, so did the frogs."

"Well, I'm really thankful losing your shoes was the only bad thing that happened once you got off the path," Blake said.

"Me too! I'll never wander off again, that's for sure. I already asked God to forgive me for not staying on the path. Now, give me that flashlight! I want to look at that map!"

Blake began showing Alicia the map and the trail he had discovered. Without allowing Captain Diablo—or anything else—to distract them, they could see exactly where they needed to go. And as they started on their way, they held tight to the map. They had no doubt that it held all the information they would need to find their treasure.

TO BE CONTINUED NEXT WEEK...

Discussion Questions:

Use these questions as conversation starters. Enjoy this time of heart-to-heart conversation with your children.

1. What did you think about this story?

2. What did you think of Captain Diablo? Who do you think he represents?

3. Do you ever have crazy thoughts like Blake and Alicia did?

4. In John 10:10, Jesus said, "The thief's purpose is to steal and kill and destroy. My purpose is to give them a rich and satisfying life." What does this tell us about Captain Diablo's (or Satan's) goal for us? *(Talk about Satan's desire to get us off course through fear, distractions, confusion and bad decisions.)*

5. Parents, share how you resist the devil in your own lives.

Home Bible Study for Kids • Week 3: STAY ON THE PATH

DAY 3: GIVING LESSON — HOW DO YOU SLICE IT?

 **Suggested Time:** 10 minutes

 **Offering Scripture:** Give freely and spontaneously. Don't have a stingy heart. —Deuteronomy 15:10 MSG

 **Teacher Tip:** If you have a whole pie, let several sets of siblings be a part of your "behavioral experiment" simultaneously.

Supplies: ☐ A pie, ☐ Small plates, ☐ Knife to cut pie, ☐ Forks

Prior to Lesson:

Serve up slices of pie, one per child. Make sure one of the slices is larger than the others.

Place the pie on a table.

Lesson Instructions:

Today, I'm really excited about getting our offering ready because I'm experimenting with this nice, big piece of pie, and I like pie!

Do you like pie?

Actually, as much as I'd like to, I am not going to be the one eating this pie. You are.

(To the youngest child) Pick one piece of pie for yourself and hand the others to your brother(s)/sister(s).

(This can go one of two ways. If the Cadet gave himself/herself the bigger portion and left the smaller piece for the other child, just have fun with it, talking about how as brothers and sisters—or just people in general—it's not uncommon to want the bigger half. If it went the other direction, commend the server on his/her effort to give the other child the biggest share.)

We've had some fun here, but you know, even something this simple can let us know where our hearts are. Ask yourselves, "If that had been me, what would I have done?" In Deuteronomy 15:10, the Bible tells us to "give freely and spontaneously. Don't have a stingy heart." So the next time you have an opportunity to keep the big portion for yourself, remember what God's Word tells us—"give freely and don't have a stingy heart"—even when it comes to pie!

Notes: _____

_____

_____

Series: Sweet Life

Home Bible Study for Kids • Week 3: STAY ON THE PATH

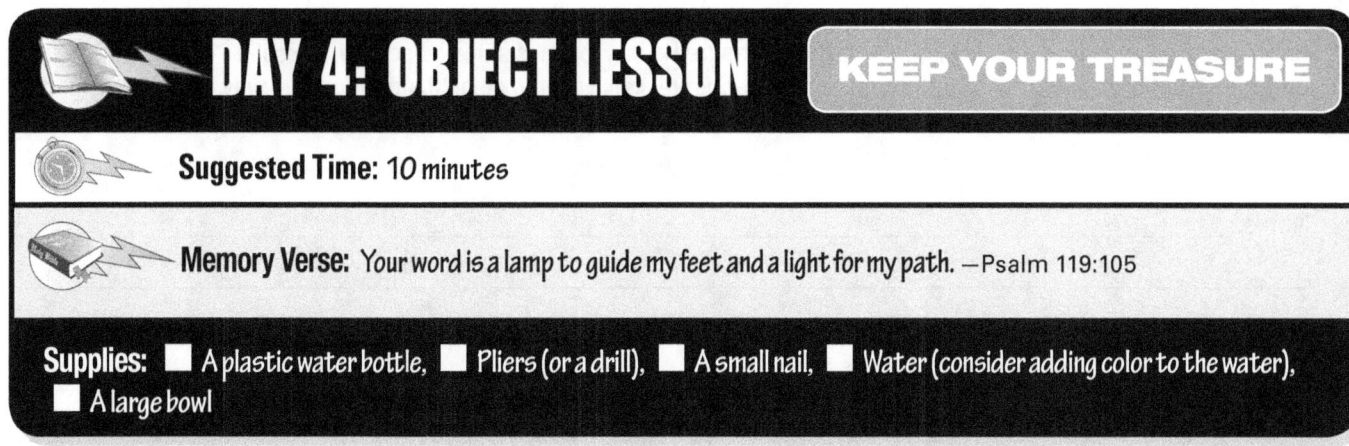

DAY 4: OBJECT LESSON — KEEP YOUR TREASURE

Suggested Time: 10 minutes

Memory Verse: Your word is a lamp to guide my feet and a light for my path. —Psalm 119:105

Supplies: ☐ A plastic water bottle, ☐ Pliers (or a drill), ☐ A small nail, ☐ Water (consider adding color to the water), ☐ A large bowl

Prior to Lesson:

Using a drill or pliers and a nail, create about 12 holes in the bottom of a plastic water bottle.

If using pliers, grip the nail with the pliers and push the nail point into the bottom of the plastic bottle to create the holes.

Once the holes have been made, fill a large bowl full of water. (Color can be added to water.) It's good to test your "treasure chest" before showing the kids.

Holding the bottle over the bowl, put enough water in the bottle to check water drainage from the holes. If the water does not drain out properly, enlarge the holes in the bottom of the bottle.

Once the water is properly draining from the bottle, refill the bottle with water and while the bottle is submerged in the bowl, place the lid on top.

Turn the bottle upright, and lift it out of the water. Water will stay in the bottle when lifted in an upright position, with the cap twisted securely on.

Lesson Instructions:

Did you know that where there's a treasure, there are plenty of treasure thieves around?

Years ago, treasure thieves were called pirates. Well, there are still pirates around today! *(Display the empty plastic bottle [with the lid off] for your children to see.)*

We'll call this plastic bottle our "treasure chest."

God's Word teaches us in 2 Corinthians 4:7 that there's treasure inside each of us, and that treasure is the glory of Jesus. We're actually much better treasure containers than this bottle, but this bottle can teach us something about holding treasure. *(Show your children the holes in the bottom of the bottle.)*

As you can see, this container may have problems holding water. So, we'll call this treasure container doing things "our way." Let's see…

(Now, hold the filled bottle upright over the bowl, without the lid, and the water will drain out.) Wow! The water didn't take long to drain out! Let's try this again, and this time, we'll place the cap on the bottle while it's underwater. *(This time the water will stay in the bottle.)*

Doing it this way is much better. Let's call this doing things "God's way"!

Series: Sweet Life

As you can see, when we do things God's way, the treasure He has for us is safe and secure. In Psalm 119:105, we see that God uses His Word to guide us into His way. So don't let pirates talk you into doing things your own way. God's Word and His way are ALWAYS best!

Notes: _____

Home Bible Study for Kids • Week 3: STAY ON THE PATH

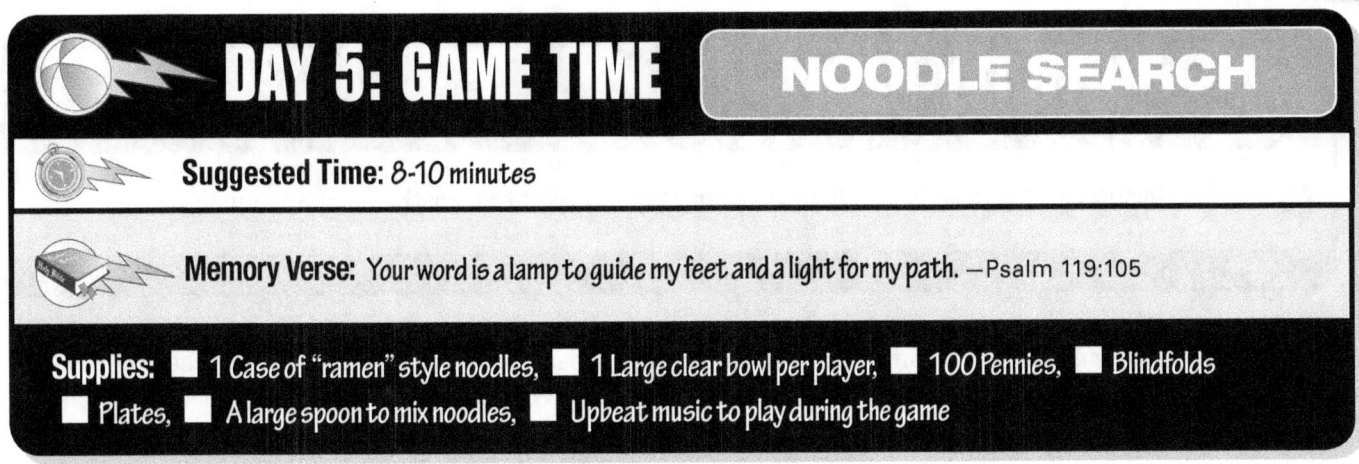

DAY 5: GAME TIME — NOODLE SEARCH

Suggested Time: 8-10 minutes

Memory Verse: Your word is a lamp to guide my feet and a light for my path. —Psalm 119:105

Supplies: ☐ 1 Case of "ramen" style noodles, ☐ 1 Large clear bowl per player, ☐ 100 Pennies, ☐ Blindfolds, ☐ Plates, ☐ A large spoon to mix noodles, ☐ Upbeat music to play during the game

Prior to Game:

Divide the ramen noodles equally into the large, clear bowls, one bowl per player. Allow the noodles to soak in water the night before.

Place the bowls of soaked noodles on a table, with a plate next to each bowl.

Divide the pennies and place an equal number in each bowl of noodles.

Stir the noodles and pennies together with a large spoon.

Players will be chosen and blindfolded. Have each player stand behind his/her bowl and face the other player(s).

Game Instructions:

Who's ready for game time?

Who's willing to wear this blindfold today?

You know, when you're blindfolded, it's a lot like being in the dark. Did you know it's a lot harder to find what you're looking for when you're in the dark? Well, to play today's game, you'll have to find pennies in the dark.

Are you up to the challenge? Let's see how well you do.

Each player will be blindfolded, and once the music starts, you'll look for the pennies in your bowl of noodles. When you find a penny, place it on the plate next to your bowl. *(To add excitement, play game music during the search.)*

Game Goal:

Whoever finds the most pennies before the music stops, wins! *(Allow 2 minutes for the game. But feel free to play several rounds.)*

Final Word:

Remember, when you shine the light of God's Word on your life, the blindfold comes off, and you'll see the good things the Father has in store for you!

Series: Sweet Life

Home Bible Study for Kids • Week 3: STAY ON THE PATH

ACTIVITY PAGE — TREASURE HUNT

Memory Verse: Your word is a lamp to guide my feet and a light for my path. —Psalm 119:105

This week, you learned just how important it is to follow the Bible. It leads to the ultimate treasure—a successful life in Jesus and THE BLESSING. Now, learn what the Bible says about God's Word. Look up these scriptures to fill in what God says about His Word.

TREASURE HUNT

- In the beginning the _____ already existed. The _____ was with God, and the _____ was God. John 1:1

- Your word is a _____ to guide my feet and a _____ for my path. Psalm 119:105

- For the word of God is alive and powerful. It is sharper than the sharpest two-edged _____, cutting between soul and spirit, between joint and marrow. It exposes our innermost thoughts and desires. Hebrews 4:12

- So the Word became _____ and made his home among us. He was full of unfailing love and faithfulness. And we have seen his glory, the glory of the Father's one and only Son. John 1:14

- And now you Gentiles have also heard the _____, the Good News that God saves you. And when you believed in Christ, he identified you as his own by giving you the Holy Spirit, whom he promised long ago. Ephesians 1:13

- For you have been born again, but not to a life that will quickly end. Your new life will last _____ because it comes from the eternal, living word of God. 1 Peter 1:23

- The grass withers and the flowers fade, but the word of our God _____ forever. Isaiah 40:8

- How can a young person stay pure? By _____ your word. Psalm 119:9

- ...People do not live by _____ alone; rather, we live by every word that comes from the mouth of the Lord. Deuteronomy 8:3

- The seed that fell on good soil represents those who truly hear and understand God's word and produce a _____ of thirty, sixty, or even a hundred times as much as had been planted! Matthew 13:23

ANSWER KEY

John 1:1: Word, Word, Word
Psalm 119:105: lamp, light
Hebrews 4:12: sword
John 1:14: flesh or human
Ephesians 1:13: truth
1 Peter 1:23: forever
Isaiah 40:8: stands
Psalm 119:9: obeying
Deuteronomy 8:3: bread
Matthew 13:23: harvest

Series: Sweet Life

WEEK 4: SELL OUT!

- **DAY 1: BIBLE LESSON—THE CALLING OF THE FIRST DISCIPLES** ▸ PG 58

- **DAY 2: READ-ALOUD—MAP KEEPERS—PROTECT YOUR TREASURE** ▸ PG 60

- **DAY 3: GIVING LESSON—STRAIGHT FROM THE HEART** ▸ PG 62

- **DAY 4: REAL DEAL—CHRISTOPHER COLUMBUS** ▸ PG 63

- **DAY 5: GAME TIME—BANANA RELAY** ▸ PG 66

- **BONUS: ACTIVITY PAGE—UNSCRAMBLED TREASURE** ▸ PG 67

**Memory Verse:** The Kingdom of Heaven is like a treasure that a man discovered hidden in a field. In his excitement, he hid it again and sold everything he owned to get enough money to buy the field. —Matthew 13:44

Home Bible Study for Kids • Week 4: SELL OUT!

WEEK 4: SNAPSHOT — SELL OUT!

DAY	TYPE OF LESSON	LESSON TITLE	SUPPLIES
Day 1	Bible Lesson	The Calling of the First Disciples	None
Day 2	Read-Aloud	Map Keepers—Protect Your Treasure	None
Day 3	Giving Lesson	Straight From the Heart	1 Dollar bill, Purse or wallet the kids will not recognize as yours, containing a $20 or $50 bill
Day 4	Real Deal	Christopher Columbus	**Optional costume/prop:** Old-fashioned captain's hat (can be found at costume stores, possibly a thrift store or can be made creatively from an inexpensive hat found in a variety store), Ruffled button-up shirt (can be found at thrift or costume stores), Black slacks, Old-fashioned knickers or rolled-up capri pants, White knee socks, Telescope (a toy one will suffice)
Day 5	Game Time	Banana Relay	2 Small trash cans, 10 Chairs, 6 Bananas, Upbeat music
Bonus	Activity Page	Unscrambled Treasure	1 Copy for each child

Lesson Introduction:

Have your children repeat this after you: "There is nothing better than the plan of God for me. There is nothing I want more than The Sweet Life He's designed for me to live."

Help your children see that the choices they make tell the truth about what is important to them. If playing a video game is chosen over obeying their parents' instructions to turn off the TV, then they have chosen the pirate, not the plan. If they "pay back" a sibling by hitting them, then revenge is more important than the Word of God that tells them to walk in love. Take a few moments to have the kids name some things that have tried to take the place of God in their lives. Every choice is an important decision that either takes them closer to the plan of God or drives them in a different direction.

Some people think this is too much for kids to understand, but it isn't! Spiritual maturity has nothing to do with chronological age. If we can train our kids to make this commitment now, they will make decisions based on the wisdom of God inside them (instead of their own desires) for the rest of their lives. They will make God-directed decisions and will experience God-empowered results!

Love,
Commander Kellie
Commander Kellie

Series: Sweet Life

Lesson Outline:

Now is the time to train your children how good the life is that God has for them—and because of God's great love for them, why they should "sell out" to Him. By selling out to God, your children will protect their relationship with Him by allowing only godly things in their lives and by surrounding themselves with like-minded friends. The Sweet Life is real, and your children need to make the decision to do whatever it takes to have it!

I. THE KINGDOM OF HEAVEN IS THE SWEET LIFE

    a. God has a good plan, a treasure, for every person who has ever lived.

    b. Is there anything you wouldn't let go of to have that treasure?

    c. A treasure seeker has to sell out, holding nothing back.

II. GUARD YOUR HEART, PROTECT YOUR TREASURE Proverbs 4:19-27

    a. Run away from evil people (and things)—don't follow their pathway! Proverbs 4:14-15

    b. Their pathway leads to destruction, sickness, sadness, fear and death.

    c. Treasure hunt with godly friends! 2 Timothy 2:22

III. WHAT WILL YOU GIVE UP FOR THIS TREASURE? Matthew 13:44

    a. Jesus paid the highest price for your Sweet Life.

    b. Keep your eyes on the prize He has for you. Philippians 3:14

    c. Don't let anything be more valuable than the plan of God for your life. Sell out! 1 John 5:21

Notes: _____

_____

_____

_____

_____

_____

_____

_____

Home Bible Study for Kids • Week 4: SELL OUT!

DAY 1: BIBLE LESSON — THE CALLING OF THE FIRST DISCIPLES

Memory Verse: The Kingdom of Heaven is like a treasure that a man discovered hidden in a field. In his excitement, he hid it again and sold everything he owned to get enough money to buy the field. —Matthew 13:44

Throughout this study, you are teaching your children about The Sweet Life that God has for them. When your children make the quality decision to follow Jesus and entrust their lives to Him, to heed the Holy Spirit and immerse themselves in the Word of God, their lives will be different. This week, they will study the parables Jesus used to describe the life of a faithful believer. Trust the Holy Spirit to bring these stories alive to your children, and give them a deeper revelation of what The Sweet Life truly is.

Read Matthew 13:44-50:
Parables of the Hidden Treasure and the Pearl

The Kingdom of Heaven is like a treasure that a man discovered hidden in a field. In his excitement, he hid it again and sold everything he owned to get enough money to buy the field.

Again, the Kingdom of Heaven is like a merchant on the lookout for choice pearls. When he discovered a pearl of great value, he sold everything he owned and bought it!

Parable of the Fishing Net

Again, the Kingdom of Heaven is like a fishing net that was thrown into the water and caught fish of every kind. When the net was full, they dragged it up onto the shore, sat down, and sorted the good fish into crates, but threw the bad ones away. That is the way it will be at the end of the world. The angels will come and separate the wicked people from the righteous, throwing the wicked into the fiery furnace, where there will be weeping and gnashing of teeth.

Discussion Questions:

1. **What was Jesus teaching His disciples about in this passage?**
   He was teaching them about the kingdom of heaven.

2. **What is the kingdom of heaven?**
   In this passage, the kingdom of heaven refers to the life we have in Jesus. It is our acceptance into and position in the family of God.

3. **To what did Jesus compare the kingdom of heaven?**
   He compared it to a treasure, a merchant looking for pearls and a fishing net.

4. **What was similar about these stories?**
   All the stories talk about people who were looking for something, and what they discovered was even greater than the people imagined.

Series: Sweet Life

5. **What can we learn about the kingdom of heaven from these stories?**
   The kingdom of heaven is a treasure to be sought after and valued. In fact, it is the most valuable thing we can ever find.

6. **Why do you think Jesus used parables, or vivid stories, to teach the disciples?**
   He used parables as a way to teach about difficult subjects so they were easier to understand.

Variation: Writing a Parable

Jesus often used parables, or picturesque stories, to teach spiritual lessons. This week, allow your older children to write their own parable on a subject of their choosing, like giving or sharing or even something funny, like getting along with a sibling.

Be sure to explain that parables usually have three components:

1. Their purpose is to make a difficult subject more understandable.

2. They use a story, as Jesus did in the above passage.

3. They compare something challenging to something more typical (for example: Jesus' comparison of the kingdom of heaven to a treasure in a field).

Notes: _____

_____
_____
_____
_____
_____
_____
_____
_____
_____
_____
_____
_____
_____
_____
_____
_____
_____
_____
_____

Home Bible Study for Kids • Week 4: SELL OUT!

DAY 2: READ-ALOUD — MAP KEEPERS—PROTECT YOUR TREASURE

 **Suggested Time:** 15 minutes

 **Memory Verse:** The Kingdom of Heaven is like a treasure that a man discovered hidden in a field. In his excitement, he hid it again and sold everything he owned to get enough money to buy the field. —Matthew 13:44

Story:

Blake stood holding the treasure map, while his friend Alicia carefully shined the flashlight onto the map's tattered edges. Meanwhile, the sinister Captain Diablo began creeping up behind them with a wicked glint in his steely eyes. Blake and Alicia were so engrossed in the details of their map, they were completely unaware of the danger lurking in the nearby shadows.

Blake spoke softly, "We're getting close. According to the map, the treasure should be right over there. This is so exciting! All our hard work is finally going to pay off!"

"I know!" Alicia said in a hushed tone. "Once we find the treasure, I can actually take a long, warm shower!"

Blake released his hold on the map to continue his search. "Alicia, look! What's that?" he asked as he uncovered gnarly vines hiding the treasure chest.

"It's a treasure chest! We've found it! Quick, open it, open it!" Alicia said excitedly.

Blake did as she said and then stopped short as he gazed on the chest's contents. "Huh. That's funny. It's just an old Bible."

As Blake processed his discovery, Captain Diablo pulled out a big bag of chocolate coins and waved them temptingly in front of Alicia and Blake. First, he held a coin up to Blake and then to Alicia.

"Ooooohh, chocolate coins," Alicia sighed contentedly, enjoying the welcome treat. "Yummy. I looooooooove chocolate!"

Blake nodded, "Yeah, I didn't realize how hungry I was until I started eating."

Captain Diablo, still silent and grinning his wicked smile, motioned to Blake to hand over the Bible in exchange for the rest of his bag of chocolate coins.

Blake looked at Alicia. "What's he saying? Do you get this?"

Alicia nodded, "Sure. I think he wants us to trade the Bible for the chocolate coins."

"I bet he could tell we were hungry," Blake laughed. "He looks like something out of a bad movie. Let's do it! Who wants this old Book anyway?"

Alicia paused, "Wait a minute! Not so fast. Why would someone go to all this trouble just to hide a Bible? Something's going on. There must be a reason it was hidden in a treasure chest. C'mon, you're great at decoding and deciphering things. I'm sure you can figure this out!"

Blake groaned, "But, I'm so hungry. I'm all 'thinked out.'"

"Blake," Alicia shot back, "you're ignoring what I'm saying. I think this pirate is trying to trick us. Besides, if he really cared about us being hungry, he wouldn't give us a bag full of chocolate coins. He would have brought us something healthier than this!"

Captain Diablo still hadn't spoken a word, but instead shook his head innocently and extended the bag of chocolate coins in

Series: Sweet Life

Blake's direction, blatantly ignoring Alicia's protests.

Blake glanced at Alicia and then, turning to decline Captain Diablo's offer, said, "Listen, Pal, until we find out exactly what's going on, there's no deal."

While Blake spoke to the old pirate, Alicia grabbed the Bible from Blake's open hand. "Look," she exclaimed, "a page is marked. I wonder why?"

Captain Diablo began pacing nervously, jingling the chocolate coins and making a nuisance of himself. Alicia ignored him while Blake tried to decipher the map's meaning. "Hmmmm, well, the map said M1344. Maybe the 'M' stands for 'Matthew.' Isn't that a book in the Bible, or at least a person's name from the Bible?"

Alicia, relieved that her friend was finally listening to her, smiled at him. "Hey, I bet you're on to something. Let me see if I can find Matthew." She started flipping erratically through the old Book. "Hmmmm, here's Matthew!"

Blake laughed, "I'm having fun again, aren't you?" He studied the map once more. "Huh...M1344, M1344. Does the page have those numbers on it somewhere?"

Alicia giggled, "There are numbers everywhere. It looks like there's a pattern though. The big numbers divide the pages and they start all over with 1 each time a big number changes. Maybe it's like chapters in a regular book or something. YES! Here's 11, 12, 13. Uh, huh. I see 42, 43, 44. Got it! It says, 'The Sweet Life is the most valuable treasure ever, and to sell everything to get it!' What's that supposed to mean?"

Blake turned to glare at Captain Diablo, who'd already begun slinking away, tiptoeing through the sand. "Now we know why Captain Diablo wanted to get this Bible out of our hands."

"We do?"

"Of course!" Blake answered quickly. "God's Word is the REAL map to lead us to the treasure."

Alicia raised her eyebrows quizzically at Blake. "Wooooooooah. Cool...I think, but I still don't get it. So what is the real treasure?"

Blake chuckled at her comical expression, "What else could it be but The Sweet Life—God's plan for our lives!"

"Ohhhhhhh," Alicia drawled, "I *do* get it. And that's why it's important to protect our walk with God at any cost!

"Beat it, Captain Diablo!" she yelled at his retreating form. "No number of worthless chocolate coins is worth giving up *this* treasure!"

THE END

Discussion Questions:

Use these questions as conversation starters. Enjoy this time of heart-to-heart conversation with your children.

1. Why was Captain Diablo trying to distract Blake and Alicia?

2. How did he try to distract them? What were his methods?

3. Matthew 13:44 says, "The Kingdom of Heaven is like a treasure that a man discovered hidden in a field. In his excitement, he hid it again and sold everything he owned to get enough money to buy the field." What does that scripture mean to you?

4. Why is God's Word so valuable?

5. Parents, share why God's Word is so valuable to you.

Home Bible Study for Kids • Week 4: SELL OUT!

DAY 3: GIVING LESSON — STRAIGHT FROM THE HEART

Suggested Time: 10 minutes

Offering Scripture: You must each decide in your heart how much to give. And don't give reluctantly or in response to pressure. "For God loves a person who gives cheerfully." —2 Corinthians 9:7

Supplies: ☐ 1 Dollar bill, ☐ Purse or wallet the kids will not recognize as yours, containing a $20 or $50 bill

Lesson Instructions:

I don't know about you, but I'm really looking forward to giving in the offering at church on Sunday. In fact, I have had this dollar set aside to give *(take dollar bill out of your pocket and show to the kids)* all week. The only thing is I would like to give more than just $1. So…check this out: I found somebody's purse when we were at the park *(or somewhere else believable)*, and thought I'd see if maybe there was some money in here, that way I could give a bigger offering. *(Start rummaging through the purse and find the bigger bill.)*

Oh great! Look at this, a $20 bill! Now I have a better offering to give. What do you think? Isn't this a good idea, since I want to give more to God than just this dollar? *(Let the kids set you straight.)* I was just testing you, but listen to how God thinks about the way we give our offerings.

Second Corinthians 9:7 says, "You must each decide in your heart how much to give. And don't give reluctantly or in response to pressure. 'For God loves a person who gives cheerfully.'"

Does this verse say to give a huge offering? Does it say to give a tiny one? Does the size of your offering matter to God?

What matters the most to God about our offerings?

What this verse tells me is that my attitude is the most important thing to God. Let's decide in our hearts right now that we are going to be cheerful givers today, and especially at church!

Notes: _____

_____

_____

_____

_____

_____

_____

_____

Series: Sweet Life

Home Bible Study for Kids • Week 4: SELL OUT!

DAY 4: REAL DEAL — CHRISTOPHER COLUMBUS

 **Memory Verse:** The Kingdom of Heaven is like a treasure that a man discovered hidden in a field. In his excitement, he hid it again and sold everything he owned to get enough money to buy the field. —Matthew 13:44

 **Concept:** Highlighting an interesting historical place, figure or event that illustrates the theme of the day. The theme of the day is turning your back on everything else to pursue God's plan.

 **Media:** If you have the technical capability, show media photos of Christopher Columbus. If you do not have this capability, you may print out photos from the Internet to show the kids or check out a book from your local library.

 **Teacher Tip:** This segment has many possible variations. Choose the one that best fits your family, and have fun!

Optional Costume/Prop: ☐ Old-fashioned captain's hat (can be found at costume stores, possibly a thrift store or can be made creatively from an inexpensive hat found in a variety store), ☐ Ruffled button-up shirt (can be found at thrift or costume stores), ☐ Black slacks, ☐ Old-fashioned knickers or rolled-up capri pants, ☐ White knee socks, ☐ Telescope (a toy one will suffice)

Intro:

We've been talking for several weeks about finding the best treasure of all—God's plan for our lives. When it comes to finding treasure, real treasure hunters hold nothing back.

Speaking of holding nothing back, one man was so fearless that he became one of the greatest explorers of all time. They called him the "Admiral of the Ocean Sea." He didn't set out to be a treasure hunter, but ended up finding one, anyway. In Spanish, his name is Cristóbal Colón.

Lesson Instructions:

Christopher Columbus was born in Genoa, Italy, in October 1451. No one knows the exact date because during that time in Italy, birthdays weren't celebrated, just special feast days. The feast day a child celebrated depended on the saint he or she was named after. Christopher was named after "Saint Christopher," who was called the saint of travelers.

Little did Christopher's parents know that their boy would become one of the most famous travelers of all time! He was called the "Admiral of the Ocean Sea."

A Big Challenge:

Most people know about Christopher Columbus because he is famous for being the one who "discovered" the Americas, but that wasn't even his goal! He was really searching for a new way to sail to India, China and Japan. For over 200 years, people in Europe traded supplies with people in Asia, but around the year 1450, the path was filled with great dangers from hostile armies and almost completely impassable. Sailors began searching for a new route to Asia, which was called the

Series: Sweet Life

Home Bible Study for Kids • Week 4: SELL OUT!

Far East. Some tried to sail around the tip of Africa, but that was also long, difficult and dangerous. Columbus was convinced the earth was round, not flat, as almost everyone in his day believed. They thought that if you sailed too far in one direction, you would fall off the edge of the earth. Since, by his calculations, Christopher knew the earth was most surely round, he decided to try something no one else had ever done. If the earth were really round, as he believed, he would be able to sail west across the Atlantic Ocean and be able to reach India and the Far East.

Christopher Columbus was moving against the cultural beliefs of his day during his efforts at exploration. His primary occupation was not a sailor, even though he did have a great deal of naval experience. He was really a map maker—a *cartographer*—well-educated, who read incessantly. He was inspired by the writings of Marco Polo to discover an ocean trade route between Asia and Europe, rather than the preferred route of his day which was by land. But, there were many obstacles. Many of the assumptions other educated men of his time made about traveling the ocean included these unusual ideas. People believed:

1. There were places in the ocean where the water reached boiling temperatures, and this could cause ships to catch on fire.

2. Monsters were waiting to attack the captains and crew.

3. The ocean was way too immense to cross.

4. If a ship sailed west, it would go downhill, meaning the ship could never return home since uphill sailing would be impossible.

5. Most people thought the world was flat and that they would sail off the edge into the unknown if they went too far, much like something falling off the edge of a table.

The Ultimate Treasure Hunt:

Despite these obstacles, Christopher refused to be afraid. He met with a great deal of opposition, and his appeals were turned down repeatedly by the influential kings and queens of his day. He approached the kings of France and Portugal, but they wouldn't help him get the ships he needed to make the long voyage. But, when he approached the king and queen of Spain, at first, Queen Isabella denied his request, but later she and King Ferdinand decided to finance his trip to what is now known as the Americas. Since the ships came from the king and queen, they were state-of-the-art for that day! So, in 1492, Christopher Columbus set out to find another path to the Far East, little knowing he would pave the way to the amazing treasure of greater knowledge of the earth as well as discover a great, new land.

Christopher Columbus returned home to tell everyone of his discovery. When he arrived back in Spain, he also told the people that he didn't see any sea monsters or boiling waters anywhere on his long trip! Because of his voyage, many wrong ideas of his day were made right. He was able to contradict the common belief that there was only one ocean and three continents.

Columbus' bravery and discovery encouraged many sailors to join him and follow in his footsteps. Christopher and his crews sailed for a total of four voyages, including exploration of present day Haiti, the Dominican Republic, Cuba, Puerto Rico, Venezuela, Argentina, Mexico, Honduras and Panama. Columbus' fourth and final voyage was dubbed the "High Voyage" because it was the fastest ocean crossing, made in a mere 21 days. On this trip, he discovered what is now Honduras, Nicaragua, Costa Rica, Panama and Martinique. Because of the power entrusted to Columbus by King Ferdinand and Queen Isabella, Columbus actually governed the lands he was exploring for Spain. In fact, one of his voyages included more than 1200 men! From mapmaker to governor and admiral is quite a journey!

Outro:

All over the world, people still celebrate Christopher Columbus' brave discoveries. In most states in the U.S., the first voyage and the discovery of America is celebrated on Columbus Day, recognizing the man who took paths no one had yet explored to connect Europe to an amazing new land. So, whenever the second Monday in October rolls around, you can celebrate by doing something new and brave! Hopefully, you'll follow Christopher Columbus' example and travel the path God has for you, even if you can't see the destination! Christopher Columbus held nothing back, and he discovered new lands, treasures and God's great adventure for his life. That's why Christopher Columbus is today's Real Deal.

Variation No. 1: Photos

Have pictures (from a book or website) available to add context to the time period of Christopher Columbus.

Variation No. 2: Map Skills

Have your kids locate on a world map each place that Columbus visited in his journeys, or print a blank world map from the Internet and color the countries. Color the countries he visited on his first journey red, his second journey blue, his third journey yellow, and his fourth journey green.

Notes: _____
_____
_____
_____
_____
_____
_____
_____
_____
_____
_____
_____
_____
_____
_____
_____
_____
_____
_____
_____

Home Bible Study for Kids • Week 4: SELL OUT!

DAY 5: GAME TIME — BANANA RELAY

Suggested Time: 10 minutes

Memory Verse: The Kingdom of Heaven is like a treasure that a man discovered hidden in a field. In his excitement, he hid it again and sold everything he owned to get enough money to buy the field. —Matthew 13:44

Supplies: ☐ 2 Small trash cans, ☐ 10 Chairs, ☐ 6 Bananas, ☐ Upbeat music to play during the game

Prior to Game:

Arrange chairs in 2 lines, with 5 chairs in each line. Consider moving the game outside or into a garage for space or to keep concerns about mess to a minimum.

Place a trash can near each chair line, leaving plenty of room for the kids to run around the chairs.

Game Instructions:

Choose 2 teams.

Review the memory verse together.

Each player must pick a seat, but choose 1 person for each team to be first who likes bananas.

Give a banana to the player in chair No. 1 of each team. When the music starts, each player passes the banana to the next player, until it reaches the end of the row. The banana must be passed to each player and then returned to the front. Once it reaches the end of the line, the player in the last chair carries the banana behind the group and sits in the first chair, forcing everyone to move back 1 chair. Keep repeating this until the original player in chair No. 1 has returned.

The player in chair No. 1 peels and puts the entire banana in his or her mouth. Be ready with trash cans for banana spills!

Game Goal:

The first team to eat the entire banana, wins.

Variation No. 1: 1 Team

Have 1 team, but try to beat the clock.

Variation No. 2: Cheese and Crackers

If your kids don't like bananas or you need a less messy option, try squeezing spreadable cheese onto a cracker and eating the entire cracker after passing it through the team.

Series: Sweet Life

Home Bible Study for Kids • Week 4: SELL OUT!

 **ACTIVITY PAGE** — UNSCRAMBLED TREASURE

 **Memory Verse:** The Kingdom of Heaven is like a treasure that a man discovered hidden in a field. In his excitement, he hid it again and sold everything he owned to get enough money to buy the field. —Matthew 13:44

In this week's Bible Lesson, Jesus used parables to teach His disciples about the kingdom of Heaven. His stories helped unscramble the meaning and value of living a faithful Christian life. And now it's your turn to do some unscrambling. Unscramble these words from the Bible Lesson passage, Matthew 14:44-50.

SAEERURT _ _ _ _ _ _ _ _
GDMONIK   _ _ _ _ _ _ _
SHIFGNI   _ _ _ _ _ _ _
DEFLI   _ _ _ _ _
LREASP   _ _ _ _ _ _
DEHIDN   _ _ _ _ _ _
AELRBAP   _ _ _ _ _ _ _
RATEW   _ _ _ _ _
CHMETNAR _ _ _ _ _ _ _ _
SHFI   _ _ _ _

Series: Sweet Life

Home Bible Study for Kids • Week 4: SELL OUT!

Answer Key

TREASURE
KINGDOM
FISHING
FIELD
PEARLS
HIDDEN
PARABLE
WATER
MERCHANT
FISH

Notes:

WEEK 5: ALL OF MY HEART

- DAY 1: BIBLE LESSON—SAMUEL ANOINTS DAVID ▶ PG 72

- DAY 2: READ-ALOUD—B-RAD'S EXCELLENT ADVENTURE, PART 1: "THE NAME CHANGE" ▶ PG 74

- DAY 3: GIVING LESSON—SUPERKIDS ARE ALWAYS PREPARED ▶ PG 76

- DAY 4: FOOD FUN—THE REAL THING ▶ PG 78

- DAY 5: GAME TIME—WITH ALL YOUR HEART ▶ PG 79

- BONUS: ACTIVITY PAGE—SEEING WHAT'S REAL ▶ PG 81

 **Memory Verse:** And you must love the Lord your God with all your heart, all your soul, and all your strength. —Deuteronomy 6:5

Home Bible Study for Kids • Week 5: ALL OF MY HEART

WEEK 5: SNAPSHOT — ALL OF MY HEART

DAY	TYPE OF LESSON	LESSON TITLE	SUPPLIES
Day 1	Bible Lesson	Samuel Anoints David	None
Day 2	Read-Aloud	B-Rad's Excellent Adventure, Part 1: "The Name Change"	None
Day 3	Giving Lesson	Superkids Are Always Prepared	Beach items: Magazines, Sunglasses, Towels, Ice chest, Picnic basket, Swim "floaties," Snorkel, Sand toys, etc. (the more creative the supplies, the better), Heavy winter clothing
Day 4	Food Fun	The Real Thing	3-4 Slices of processed American cheese food, 1 Loaf of processed cheese product, Several varieties of gourmet cheeses, Plates
Day 5	Game Time	With All Your Heart	1 Flannel board, Easel, Hearts cut from felt, Small candy or prizes, Upbeat music
Bonus	Activity Page	Seeing What's Real	1 Copy for each child

Lesson Introduction:

This is a perfect lesson to invite your children to make a decision for God. Even those who have accepted Jesus as their Lord and Savior can make a greater commitment to withhold nothing from Him. Make this the day you submit everything to God. Invite your children to pray with you.

I would lead them in a simple prayer similar to this example: "Dear God, thank You for making us free! You never force us to serve You, but Your Word says that if we do, You will bless us. Today, we are telling You that our hearts belong to You, 100 percent. We love You and will serve You with all that we have. Thank You for being our great and wonderful heavenly Father!"

Commander Dana
—Commander Dana

Home Bible Study for Kids • Week 5: ALL OF MY HEART

Lesson Outline:

In this week's lesson, you will train your children to follow the Lord with their whole hearts—not only on Sundays, or only in church-related issues—but in *everything*. God loves your children enough to give them a free will, but He desires for them to follow Him passionately, not holding anything back. When they do that, they will be strong in Him—spirit, soul and body.

I. YOUR HEART IS THE REAL YOU

a. God created us to be like Him—in His exact image. Genesis 1:26

b. Our heavenly Father is an eternal spirit, and so are we.

c. The Bible calls our spirit our "heart." Our heart is the most important part of who we are!

II. WHAT GOD SEES 1 SAMUEL 16:7

a. The prophet Samuel thought he was surely looking at Israel's new king.

b. David's brother Eliab was tall and handsome.

c. God looked at Eliab's heart and said, "No way!"

d. When God saw David's heart, He saw a heart that pleased Him a lot.

III. WHAT GOD IS LOOKING FOR

a. Our Father lets us make our own choices. Deuteronomy 30:19-20

b. He does not force us to love Him.

c. Giving our hearts to Jesus is the only way to really love God!

d. God wants kids who have hearts that love Him and love people.

This is one of the things God loved about David. Even though David was a great warrior, he was softhearted toward people, and would defend the helpless and the righteous.

Notes: _____
_____
_____
_____
_____

Series: Sweet Life

Home Bible Study for Kids • Week 5: ALL OF MY HEART

 DAY 1: BIBLE LESSON — SAMUEL ANOINTS DAVID

 **Memory Verse:** And you must love the Lord your God with all your heart, all your soul, and all your strength. —Deuteronomy 6:5

Today's story is such a powerful lesson! Samuel, the prophet of God, thought he knew what God wanted, but even so, he still stopped and listened to what God was actually saying! When Samuel listened to the Lord, he learned something: a person's heart is much more important to God than outward appearances. There are so many ways you can apply this concept to practical life. Encourage your kids to listen to the Holy Spirit and follow the awesome example of Samuel, who realized God was looking at David's heart more than his skills and appearance.

Read 1 Samuel 16:1-13:

Now the Lord said to Samuel, "You have mourned long enough for Saul. I have rejected him as king of Israel, so fill your flask with olive oil and go to Bethlehem. Find a man named Jesse who lives there, for I have selected one of his sons to be my king."

But Samuel asked, "How can I do that? If Saul hears about it, he will kill me."

"Take a heifer with you," the Lord replied, "and say that you have come to make a sacrifice to the Lord. Invite Jesse to the sacrifice, and I will show you which of his sons to anoint for me."

So Samuel did as the Lord instructed. When he arrived at Bethlehem, the elders of the town came trembling to meet him. "What's wrong?" they asked. "Do you come in peace?"

"Yes," Samuel replied. "I have come to sacrifice to the Lord. Purify yourselves and come with me to the sacrifice." Then Samuel performed the purification rite for Jesse and his sons and invited them to the sacrifice, too.

When they arrived, Samuel took one look at Eliab and thought, "Surely this is the Lord's anointed!"

But the Lord said to Samuel, "Don't judge by his appearance or height, for I have rejected him. The Lord doesn't see things the way you see them. People judge by outward appearance, but the Lord looks at the heart."

Then Jesse told his son Abinadab to step forward and walk in front of Samuel. But Samuel said, "This is not the one the Lord has chosen." Next Jesse summoned Shimea, but Samuel said, "Neither is this the one the Lord has chosen." In the same way all seven of Jesse's sons were presented to Samuel.

But Samuel said to Jesse, "The Lord has not chosen any of these." Then Samuel asked, "Are these all the sons you have?"

"There is still the youngest," Jesse replied. "But he's out in the fields watching the sheep and goats."

"Send for him at once," Samuel said. "We will not sit down to eat until he arrives."

So Jesse sent for him. He was dark and handsome, with beautiful eyes. And the Lord said, "This is the one; anoint him."

So as David stood there among his brothers, Samuel took the flask of olive oil he had brought and anointed David with the oil. And the Spirit of the Lord came powerfully upon David from that day on. Then Samuel returned to Ramah.

Home Bible Study for Kids • Week 5: ALL OF MY HEART

Discussion Questions:

1. What did God ask Samuel to do?
He told him to quit mourning for Saul and go on a journey to anoint the new king.

2. Why didn't Samuel want to obey?
He was afraid Saul would find out about him going to anoint a new king, and his life would be endangered.

3. How did God help?
God told him to take and prepare a sacrifice to offer, and then he would be safe from Saul's questions.

4. Who did Samuel think would be the next king?
Samuel thought Jesse's oldest son, Eliab, would be crowned king.

5. Why didn't God choose him?
Eliab was rejected, not because of his appearance, but because of what was in his heart.

6. Who did God finally choose?
God chose David.

7. What was David's job?
At the time, he was a shepherd.

8. What did you learn, today, about God's opinions of people?
God values the heart, or character, much more than the outward appearance!

9. Are there things in your heart that might be like Eliab? Or, do you have a heart like David?
Answers will vary, but this is a great time to let the Holy Spirit do His work!

Variation: Journaling

Encourage children to write about why God values the state of someone's heart more than outward appearances. And, if there is a "heart issue" they would like God to help them with, then encourage them to write about that. Agree with them in prayer for the Holy Spirit to help and direct them. Let this be an open and honest time without criticism or judgment. Remember, everyone—even parents—have areas that need to be strengthened.

Notes: _____
_____
_____
_____
_____
_____
_____
_____

Series: Sweet Life

Home Bible Study for Kids • Week 5: ALL OF MY HEART

DAY 2: READ-ALOUD — B-RAD'S EXCELLENT ADVENTURE, PART 1: "THE NAME CHANGE"

 **Suggested Time:** 15 minutes

 **Memory Verse:** And you must love the Lord your God with all your heart, all your soul, and all your strength. —Deuteronomy 6:5

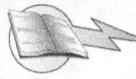 **Background:** This week begins a five-week read-aloud series, "All of Me," about a writer's discussions of his developing story with his younger friend Tyson, a surfer with a dry sense of humor, who's slightly sarcastic, but all in fun. At the end of this five-week series, the audience will discover that the "Writer" is really B-Rad himself. This story is loosely based on the life of the Apostle Paul. This story includes fun surfing lingo. The unusual terms are defined in parentheses.

Story:

An aspiring teenage author sat scribbling into a notebook while sitting at the beachfront. He was engrossed in his writing until his friend Tyson interrupted, "Hey, what's crackin'?"

The writer paused and looked at his friend, "Oh, hey, Tyson. What's up with you?"

"Well, I was going to ride the waves a bit, but these just look like ankle snappers (tiny waves that are not worth riding)," Tyson replied. "How 'bout you? What's up with the umbrella over the chair, the granny bag with sunscreen and are those, seriously, sunflower seeds in there? And the pencils and paper?"

The writer laughed good-naturedly at the teasing while extending a bag of snacks to his friend. "I'm writing a story, bro."

Grabbing a handful of the salty treat, Tyson whistled, "Whoa! Fill me in, dude! I'll say I knew you before your rise to fame and stardom."

"Actually, Tyson, that wasn't the plan at all," the writer chuckled. "I'm calling my story 'B-Rad's Excellent Adventure.' Are you sure you wanna hear this?"

Tyson, "I'd be cuccini (totally ridiculous) not to hear it straight up from you. Besides, I need something to do while I'm waiting for the surf to pick up out there. I'll be your captured, er, captivated, audience. Read on, dawg (friend). You are coolaphonic (coolest of the cool), man."

The writer began reading his introduction:

"Deep in the halls of Monroe High School was a neglected guy named Bookworm Brad, nicknamed thus because that's all he ever did—he read. But, as brilliant as B.B. was, he had one formidable problem."

At this point, Tyson interjected, "Dude, totally un-cool. Seriously? I can't relate to a guy who only likes to read. And what kind of guy gets dubbed with a name like 'Bookworm'? That's sad."

"Hey, this is *my* story, man," the writer objected. "Give it a chance."

"Totally, dude. Just sayin,' that's an awful lot of baggage to carry around. . . being a lonesome reader."

"No kidding!" the writer responded. "Shall I continue?"

Series: Sweet Life

Home Bible Study for Kids • Week 5: ALL OF MY HEART

"I'm frothing (excited, stoked, anxious), bro," Tyson replied dryly. "Seriously, I'm hooked. What's next?"

The writer dropped his shades from the top of his head to his eyes and read on.

"His problem was that he didn't know Jesus, and he hated everyone who did. He especially hated the RAD Surfers, a group of surfing kids who totally loved God and tried to follow Jesus' teachings. Bookworm Brad despised them so much that he and his friends would throw books at them and spread lies about them trying to get them kicked out of school."

Tyson responded, "Hey, dude, that's a great beginning! You're setting up for some action, methinks. Where's the fight? I bet it's going to be hugangus (very, very, big)."

"Well... Brad decided he had come up with the perfect plan to get rid of the RAD Surfers once and for all and get them into serious trouble. That's when it happened. He received a text message that changed his life forever. The text told him to go to The Coffee Shack and wait for instructions. Brad thought it was totally weird to receive this text from someone he didn't know, but thought he'd show up at The Coffee Shack and figure out who was pranking him because the text was signed by 'Jesus.'"

The writer paused for effect.

"The plot thickens!" Tyson exclaimed. "I didn't know you had it in you, man, to distract me from the waves with a book. Awesome! I can't wait to see who's really at The Coffee Shack. Can you give me the scoop, or are you going to leave me hangin'?"

"I would if I could, bro, but I haven't finished it. The basic synopsis is that no one strange is at The Coffee Shack when Brad gets there. He finds a Bible on an abandoned surfboard, opens to John 3:16, realizes the error of his ways and totally sells out to Jesus."

"Radical, man!" Tyson answered. "Who knew an imaginary character could entice me to ignore those waves that are getting juicy (good waves with power, speed and clean faces) out there."

The writer glanced up at Tyson, "Did I say Brad was imaginary?"

"You're writing a book, John (a name used for anyone in the surfing world). Of course, it's fiction. I haven't heard any real stories where Jesus sent text messages and Bibles were opened to sermons at a coffee shop. That wave out there has my name on it, and that's real. I gotta go. Chow (good-bye)."

TO BE CONTINUED NEXT WEEK...

Discussion Questions:

Use these questions as conversation starters. Enjoy this time of heart-to-heart conversation with your children.

1. Can you tell me three things that happened in this story?

2. Where does it take place?

3. What do you think of the two characters in this story—the writer and Tyson? Are they good friends? Are they Christians? What are they like?

4. What do you think of the writer's story?

Series: Sweet Life

Home Bible Study for Kids • Week 5: ALL OF MY HEART

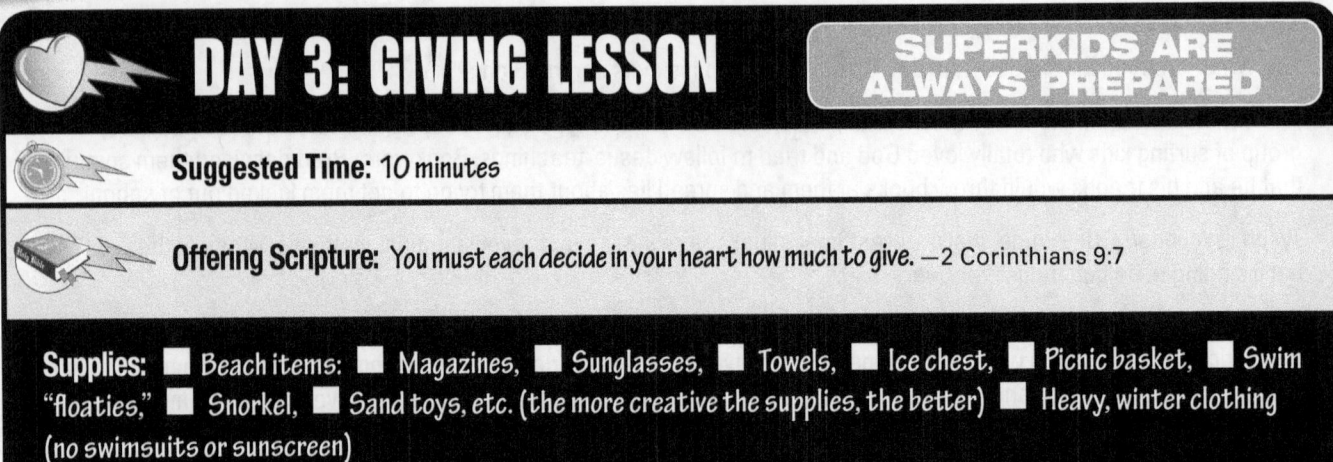

DAY 3: GIVING LESSON

SUPERKIDS ARE ALWAYS PREPARED

Suggested Time: 10 minutes

Offering Scripture: You must each decide in your heart how much to give. —2 Corinthians 9:7

Supplies: ☐ Beach items: ☐ Magazines, ☐ Sunglasses, ☐ Towels, ☐ Ice chest, ☐ Picnic basket, ☐ Swim "floaties," ☐ Snorkel, ☐ Sand toys, etc. (the more creative the supplies, the better) ☐ Heavy, winter clothing (no swimsuits or sunscreen)

Prior to Lesson:

Be prepared for the beach, with sand toys, etc., but dress up in heavy, winter clothing.

Lesson Instructions:

Wow! It's a great day for going to the beach/pool. Last week, we decided to go to the beach after church. What's not to enjoy about the beach? It's fun to play in the sand and swim.

Do you like going to the beach?

What's the best thing about going to the beach?

Well, I think we have everything we need to have a great beach day!

Would you like to see and hear about all the cool stuff we're taking and planning to do at the beach?

(Allow time to sort through the beach items.)

Is there anything we're missing?

Thanks for reminding me about sunscreen, and most importantly, my swimsuit!

It wouldn't be fun to arrive at the beach and not be able to swim in the water, or have no sunscreen and end up fried!

This reminds me of a scripture about going to church prepared. Let me ask you a few questions.

Did we make a decision about what we wanted to eat today? Did we make a decision about what clothes to wear today?

Did you make a decision to read your Bible today?

It's great to be prepared, especially when going somewhere. There are a lot of decisions to make when we get ready for church, too, and even what to do after church! Sometimes, as we prepare, we forget about a very important preparation—our offerings to the Lord and others. Second Corinthians 9:7 teaches us, "You must each decide in your heart how much to give…." God has given us The Sweet Life and so many good things to enjoy! Take time to look, listen and obey your heart and decide what to bring to church as your offering.

Series: Sweet Life

Variation: Seasons

If this lesson falls in the middle of winter, beach items will be a hassle to gather. Instead, gather items for a snow day such as snow boots, a warm coat, skis and a scarf. Just leave out the gloves and some other important item, like boots or jacket, for the same effect in your lesson.

Notes: _____

Home Bible Study for Kids • Week 5: ALL OF MY HEART

DAY 4: FOOD FUN — THE REAL THING

Suggested Time: 10 minutes

Key Scripture: People judge by outward appearance, but the Lord looks at the heart. —1 Samuel 16:7

Supplies: ☐ 3-4 Slices of processed American cheese food, ☐ 1 Loaf of processed cheese product, ☐ Several varieties of gourmet cheeses ☐ Plates (to display the cheese varieties)

Lesson Instructions:

Today, instead of making a food dish, we're going to experience a "cheese tasting."

This cheese tasting is for those who are not afraid of trying food that's different than what they're used to.

(Display the cheese varieties on several plates. Consider adding some garnish like parsley and crackers to the cheese plate. Create small cards with the name of each cheese type on the cards and place next to each cheese plate.)

The first cheese we'll try is this sliced American cheese.

Cheese testers, what do you think?

(Allow your cheese testers to taste each variety, one by one, and get their input. Place a glass of water next to each child to "cleanse their palate" after each taste. Feel free to join in tasting the cheese.)

We've had fun trying the cheese varieties, but it's not just the taste that makes cheese different. Actually, two of these so-called cheeses are impostors! That's right, two of them are not real cheese. They are called "cheese food" or "cheese products," but they're not the real thing!

Can anyone guess which two are not cheese?

That's right! The American slices and the processed cheese product loaf are processed cheese food.

Just by looking at the American slices and the processed cheese product loaf, it would be challenging to recognize they're impostors! It's the same with people. Sometimes, we can look at someone and think we know everything about them from what we see on the outside, but the Bible tells us that the real you is the person on the inside.

Want to know what God sees? Check out your heart—that's the real you!

Variation: Fruit Juice

If, for some reason, this cheese tasting will not work for your family, use juices instead. Try some fruit-flavored drinks versus the real, 100 percent juice. Use orange, grape and apple. See if the kids can figure out which is the real juice and which is just flavored to taste like the real thing.

Series: Sweet Life

Home Bible Study for Kids • Week 5: ALL OF MY HEART

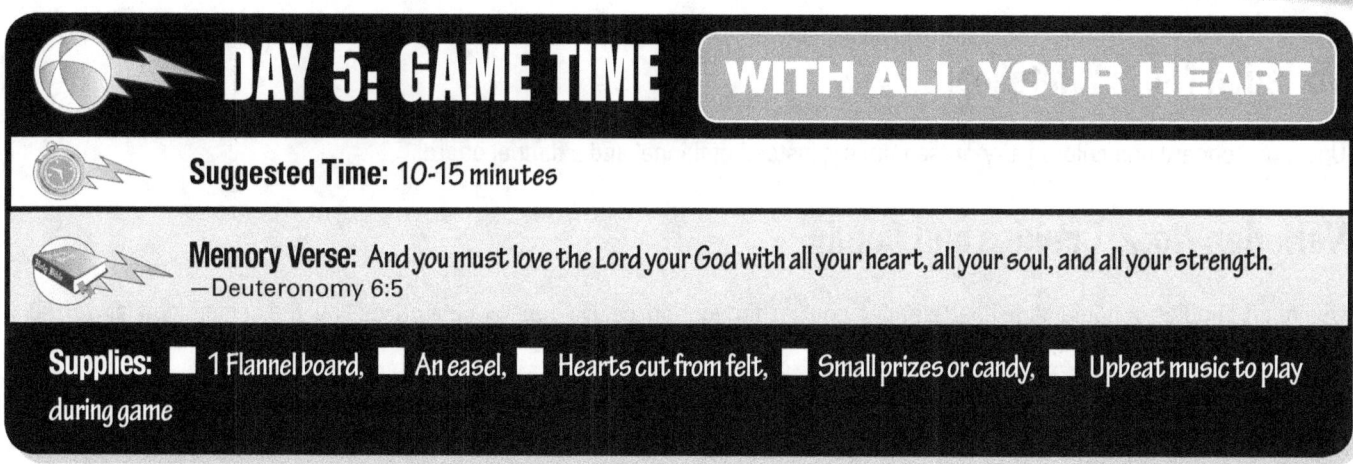

DAY 5: GAME TIME — WITH ALL YOUR HEART

Suggested Time: 10-15 minutes

Memory Verse: And you must love the Lord your God with all your heart, all your soul, and all your strength.
—Deuteronomy 6:5

Supplies: ☐ 1 Flannel board, ☐ An easel, ☐ Hearts cut from felt, ☐ Small prizes or candy, ☐ Upbeat music to play during game

Prior to Game:

Place the flannel board on an easel, and place or draw a dividing line down the middle. Choose an assistant to hold the felt hearts.

Game Instructions:

This game will test your kids' "Word-search" skills! Each contestant will need a Bible. The game leader will read a Scripture reference, and the kids will look up the verse to determine if it refers to "heart," "soul" or "strength." For example, if the key word in the verse was *strong,* the correct answer would be "strength." The first kid (or team) to find the reference and identify the correct subject, wins 1 felt heart placed on the flannel board for his/her (or team) score and a small prize or candy.

Game Goal:

The kid (or team) with the most hearts, wins!

Scripture Reference:	Answer:	Scripture Reference:	Answer:
1 Samuel 16:7	Heart	Exodus 15:2	Strength
Psalm 84:5	Strength	Hebrews 4:12	Soul
Proverbs 4:23	Heart	Proverbs 16:9	Soul
Isaiah 55:3	Soul	Matthew 16:26	Soul
Malachi 4:6	Heart	Proverbs 18:10	Strength
Matthew 6:21	Heart		

Final Word:

Learning to search God's Word teaches us about our hearts, our souls and true strength!

Series: Sweet Life

Variation No. 1: Whiteboard

Use a whiteboard and colored, dry-erase markers instead of flannel and a flannel board.

Variation No. 2: Cookies and Candy

Use heart candies or homemade heart-shaped cookies for your prizes. No eating of the prizes until the competition is over, so that you can determine who the winner is!

Variation No. 3: Young Children

For young children, read the scriptures aloud for them and let them determine whether the verse refers to heart, soul or strength.

Notes: _____
_____
_____
_____
_____
_____
_____
_____
_____
_____
_____
_____
_____
_____
_____
_____
_____
_____
_____
_____

Home Bible Study for Kids • Week 5: ALL OF MY HEART

ACTIVITY PAGE — SEEING WHAT'S REAL

Memory Verse: And you must love the Lord your God with all your heart, all your soul, and all your strength.
—Deuteronomy 6:5

This week, we've talked about having a real, sold-out heart for God. In the Bible Lesson, we saw that even though he looked good enough to be king on the outside, David's brother, Eliab, was rejected in favor of David, the youngest family member. Why? Because God knows the real from the impostor. He sees what others miss. Today, see how good your observation skills are. Below, are two pictures. At first glance, they look the same but, in fact, there are 10 differences between them. Can you find them?

Series: Sweet Life

Home Bible Study for Kids • Week 5: ALL OF MY HEART

Notes:

Series: Sweet Life

WEEK 6: ALL OF MY MIND

- DAY 1: BIBLE LESSON—CAIN AND ABEL ▶ PG 86
- DAY 2: READ-ALOUD—B-RAD'S EXCELLENT ADVENTURE, PART 2: "A NEW LANGUAGE" ▶ PG 88
- DAY 3: GIVING LESSON—A BLESSING EXPLOSION ▶ PG 90
- DAY 4: FOOD FUN—DO YOU RECOGNIZE POISON? ▶ PG 91
- DAY 5: GAME TIME—WORMS AWAY! ▶ PG 92
- BONUS: ACTIVITY PAGE—GOOD THOUGHTS CROSSWORD ▶ PG 95

Memory Verse: So letting your sinful nature control your mind leads to death. But letting the Spirit control your mind leads to life and peace. —Romans 8:6

Home Bible Study for Kids • Week 6: ALL OF MY MIND

WEEK 6: SNAPSHOT — ALL OF MY MIND

DAY	TYPE OF LESSON	LESSON TITLE	SUPPLIES
Day 1	Bible Lesson	Cain and Abel	None
Day 2	Read-Aloud	B-Rad's Excellent Adventure, Part 2: "A New Language"	None
Day 3	Giving Lesson	A Blessing Explosion	1-2 Cards per child of instant sponge animals in dissolving capsules (available inexpensively at toy stores or online), An eyedropper, 1 Bowl filled with water
Day 4	Food Fun	Do You Recognize Poison?	1 Apple, A plate, Vinegar, Bible
Day 5	Game Time	Worms Away!	2 Extra-large cans of pudding, 1 Bag of potting soil, 20-60 Gelatin-based candies shaped like worms, 4 Large clear bowls, Small trash can, Wet wipes, Upbeat music
Bonus	Activity Page	Good Thoughts Crossword	1 Copy for each child

Lesson Introduction:

There is such an all-out effort in the world today to influence the thoughts of our kids. You don't have to look very far to see worldly, fleshly, in-your-face advertising pushing ungodly ideas. How can we turn the tide of this invasive attack? We can do it by telling our kids the truth about God—straightforward and simple. Don't apologize, and don't water it down. Tell them how big God is going to show up in your family! You should lead them into an encounter with God every day. The one thing the world cannot offer is an experience with God Himself. It's time to get prepared, parents, pastors and teachers! You will be amazed at what will occur when you're walking every day with Jesus!

Commander Dana
—Commander Dana

Series: Sweet Life

Home Bible Study for Kids • Week 6: ALL OF MY MIND

Lesson Outline:

One of the greatest battlegrounds of the enemy is in the mind. From the beginning, Satan tried to twist people's thoughts and convince them of his lies. The good news is that your children aren't left helpless to his attacks. With the Word of God, they can stand strong. It takes discipline and faith, but with the Word to instruct and the Holy Spirit to guide, your children will overcome!

I. RIGHT THOUGHTS BRING LIFE

    a. God's Word says right thoughts bring life and peace. Romans 8:6

    b. We can keep out wrong imaginations. 2 Corinthians 10:5

    c. Philippians 4:8 tells us the thoughts we should think about.

II. WRONG THOUGHTS BRING DEATH

    a. The devil told Eve lies about God. Genesis 3:1-5

    b. Eve let those thoughts stay in her mind.

    c. Never let the devil tell you what to think!

III. THOUGHTS AND WORDS COME BEFORE ACTIONS

    a. Cain had angry thoughts. Genesis 4:5

    b. The wrong thoughts led to wrong words. Genesis 4:8

    c. Wrong words led to wrong actions.

Can you think of a time when you had to choose between right and wrong thoughts?

The Word of God says over and over again that choosing godly thoughts and words brings life and peace. Let's serve God with all of our mind!

Say this confession out loud with me: "I serve God with my mind. I trade in my thoughts for His thoughts. I will fill my mind with His Word. I choose thoughts filled with life!"

Notes: _____

_____

_____

_____

Series: Sweet Life

Home Bible Study for Kids • Week 6: ALL OF MY MIND

DAY 1: BIBLE LESSON — CAIN AND ABEL

Memory Verse: So letting your sinful nature control your mind leads to death. But letting the Spirit control your mind leads to life and peace. —Romans 8:6

This week's lesson deals with the issue of strife, which in this Bible passage, ends with dramatic results. Your children will see that simple thoughts can grow into life-changing actions. This is an excellent time to teach your children about how the thoughts they entertain develop into attitudes, attitudes develop into habits and habits into actions. That's why guarding their thoughts is so important to your children's health and happiness.

Read Genesis 4:1-16:

Now... Eve... became pregnant. When she gave birth to Cain, she said, "With the Lord's help, I have produced a man!" Later she gave birth to his brother and named him Abel.

When they grew up, Abel became a shepherd, while Cain cultivated the ground. When it was time for the harvest, Cain presented some of his crops as a gift to the Lord. Abel also brought a gift—the best of the firstborn lambs from his flock. The Lord accepted Abel and his gift, but he did not accept Cain and his gift. This made Cain very angry, and he looked dejected.

"Why are you so angry?" the Lord asked Cain. "Why do you look so dejected? You will be accepted if you do what is right. But if you refuse to do what is right, then watch out! Sin is crouching at the door, eager to control you. But you must subdue it and be its master."

One day Cain suggested to his brother, "Let's go out into the fields." And while they were in the field, Cain attacked his brother, Abel, and killed him.

Afterward the Lord asked Cain, "Where is your brother? Where is Abel?"

"I don't know," Cain responded. "Am I my brother's guardian?"

But the Lord said, "What have you done? Listen! Your brother's blood cries out to me from the ground! Now you are cursed and banished from the ground, which has swallowed your brother's blood. No longer will the ground yield good crops for you, no matter how hard you work! From now on you will be a homeless wanderer on the earth."

Cain replied to the Lord, "My punishment is too great for me to bear! You have banished me from the land and from your presence; you have made me a homeless wanderer. Anyone who finds me will kill me!"

The Lord replied, "No, for I will give a sevenfold punishment to anyone who kills you." Then the Lord put a mark on Cain to warn anyone who might try to kill him. So Cain left the Lord's presence and settled in the land of Nod, east of Eden.

Discussion Questions:

1. **What were Adam and Eve's first two kids' names?**
   Their names were Cain and Abel.
2. **Why was Cain so angry?**
   God liked Abel's sacrifice and didn't accept his.

Home Bible Study for Kids • Week 6: ALL OF MY MIND

3. What did God say when Cain pouted?
He warned him to watch out because sin was crouching at his door.

4. Did Cain listen to God?
No, he didn't. He invited his brother out into the field and then killed him!

5. What happened to Cain as a result of his sin?
A curse came on him, and he was forced to roam the earth with a mark on his body.

6. What does it mean for sin to "crouch at someone's door"? Can you think of an example when this would happen?
The choice of whether or not to sin is ours. If we entertain ungodliness, then it's easier for those thoughts to develop into actions. For Cain, he indulged in his anger toward his brother, and the result was murder. *(If you receive other examples, allow for reasonable answers.)*

7. Can you remember a time when it was hard to get along with a sibling?
Accept reasonable responses, and avoid petty conflicts that may arise from shared answers.

8. What can we learn from Cain? (Possible answers):
   a. We should always give God our best.
   b. We should accept correction from the Lord. Instead of accepting God's correction regarding his offering, Cain began to entertain anger.
   c. When God warns of sin, we should listen!
   d. We must take responsibility for our own actions.
   e. Our actions have consequences.

Notes: _____
_____
_____
_____
_____
_____
_____
_____
_____
_____
_____
_____
_____
_____
_____
_____

Series: Sweet Life

Home Bible Study for Kids • Week 6: ALL OF MY MIND

DAY 2: READ-ALOUD — B-RAD'S EXCELLENT ADVENTURE, PART 2: "A NEW LANGUAGE"

Suggested Time: 15 minutes

Memory Verse: So letting your sinful nature control your mind leads to death. But letting the Spirit control your mind leads to life and peace. —Romans 8:6

Background: This week continues the five-week read-aloud series, "All of Me," about a writer's discussions of his developing story with his younger friend Tyson, a surfer with a dry sense of humor, who's slightly sarcastic, but all in fun. At the end of this five-week series, the audience will discover that the "Writer" is really B-Rad himself. This story is loosely based on the life of the Apostle Paul. This story includes fun surfing lingo. The unusual terms are defined in parentheses.

Story:

"Howzit (how's it going), bro? What's crackin', man?" Tyson asked his friend, the writer.

"Didn't you ask me that last time I saw you?" the writer answered, without pausing to look up from the sentence he was frantically scribbling into his notebook.

"So, what's up with Brad at The Coffee Shack?" Tyson continued.

This time, his friend pointed the pencil directly at Tyson. "I KNEW you were hooked."

"Who wouldn't be, man? You've got Jesus sending text messages and sounding totally rad. I just want to know who was really at The Coffee Shack when Brad made his appearance. I bet a bunch of surfers jumped him! I think you were just trying to scare me with all that talk about the Bible being opened and all that. . . " his voice trailing off.

The writer looked at his friend. "Well, I didn't finish the part about the text. The rest of the message said that Brad was going to meet Andy, a hotdogger (a great performer on a surfboard) and that Andy would give him a high-five."

"So? Read on, man. I'm in!" Tyson piped up.

The writer continued, this time reading directly from the page he'd just located.

"It was hot as could be at The Coffee Shack when a super-buff surfer walks up and offers Brad a free iced mocha. Brad reaches out and gives the guy a high-five. Surfer-dude introduces himself with a, 'Hey, mahn, my tag is Andy. Are you understanding what you're reading, there?'"

Tyson commented, "Just like the text from 'Jesus.' Your story's getting strange here."

"It gets better when Brad learns that God sent Andy to help him understand Scripture and to get the bigger picture of leading other surfers to Jesus," the writer continued. "So the next task before them is for Andy to teach surf lingo to Brad, who's avoided all knowledge of surfing and anything associated with it, up to this point. Remember, he doesn't like surfers."

"I remember," Tyson said. "I gotta hand you this much: You've got a great imagination if you're going to create a surfer out of a guy like Brad who's spent his life hating surfers until now. But the surf lingo's a breeze for a bookworm like Brad. He just needs to study a bit. And when in doubt, just say "dude," "like" or "yo."

Series: Sweet Life

Home Bible Study for Kids • Week 6: ALL OF MY MIND

"Easy for you to say. But Brad has never spoken like that!" the writer said. "Brad soon learned that when he made Jesus his Lord, his heart wasn't the only thing that had to change—his mind had to be changed, too. He couldn't keep on hating surfers, or anyone, for that matter."

"So what happens next? And don't say you haven't gotten that far yet!" Tyson said.

The writer began scribbling on his notepad before showing it to Tyson. When he finally flipped it over, Tyson saw that he had written, "I haven't gotten that far, yet."

"Very funny. Well, let me know when you've written more in your book. And speaking of books, I better go hit the books myself, or I'll wipe out on tomorrow's history quiz. Later."

TO BE CONTINUED NEXT WEEK…

Discussion Questions:

Use these questions as conversation starters. Enjoy this time of heart-to-heart conversation with your children.

1. How had Brad's life changed?

2. How did his mind need to change?

3. Has God ever changed your mind about something or told you to do something new?

4. Parents, share a time when God changed your mind about something or directed you to do something that you never imagined He would.

Notes:_____
_____
_____
_____
_____
_____
_____
_____
_____
_____
_____
_____

Series: Sweet Life

Home Bible Study for Kids • Week 6: ALL OF MY MIND

DAY 3: GIVING LESSON — A BLESSING EXPLOSION

Suggested Time: 10 minutes

Offering Scripture: *Give freely and become more wealthy; be stingy and lose everything.* —Proverbs 11:24

Supplies: ☐ 1-2 Cards per child of instant sponge animals in dissolving capsules, available inexpensively at dollar stores, toy stores or online, ☐ Clear container partially filled with water, ☐ An eyedropper

Lesson Instructions:

We learned previously that God's plan is a treasure. There are so many good things God's Word says about how to live The Sweet Life. We must make sure we stay on the path of THE BLESSING. I've found another promise from God that you'll want to hear about.

Are you ready? *(Read Proverbs 11:24.)*

That's a great way to stay on the path God has for us, by giving freely. It's so easy. We give, and He makes us wealthy.

Who remembers learning about the pirates?

Stinginess is a pirate and after reading this scripture today, we want to stay far away from that pirate…right? I have some things I want to show you today. They are packaged funny, but they do something amazing when water is added. *(Show the difference between each item, from adding one drop of water to adding various amounts, until some are completely submerged. Even the time difference between each item changing is noticeable.)*

When we give freely, God can take our giving and make it explode into blessings, just like what we saw when water was added to each item! But, if we never let go of our offering, what will happen? NOTHING!

Kids, let's make a commitment today to never hold back from giving our all to God, to never be stingy and to not allow the devil to steal from us. Your Father loves you so much, that He can take even the smallest offering and make it grow. Give and watch His promise become real—a blessing explosion!

Variation: Bread

Make bread with your kids, and show them how a little bit of yeast mixed under the right conditions can make an amazing loaf of bread. This is what God does with our giving: He takes our small amount and makes it become something savory and wonderful! It's The Sweet Life!

Notes: _____
_____
_____
_____

Series: Sweet Life

Home Bible Study for Kids • Week 6: ALL OF MY MIND

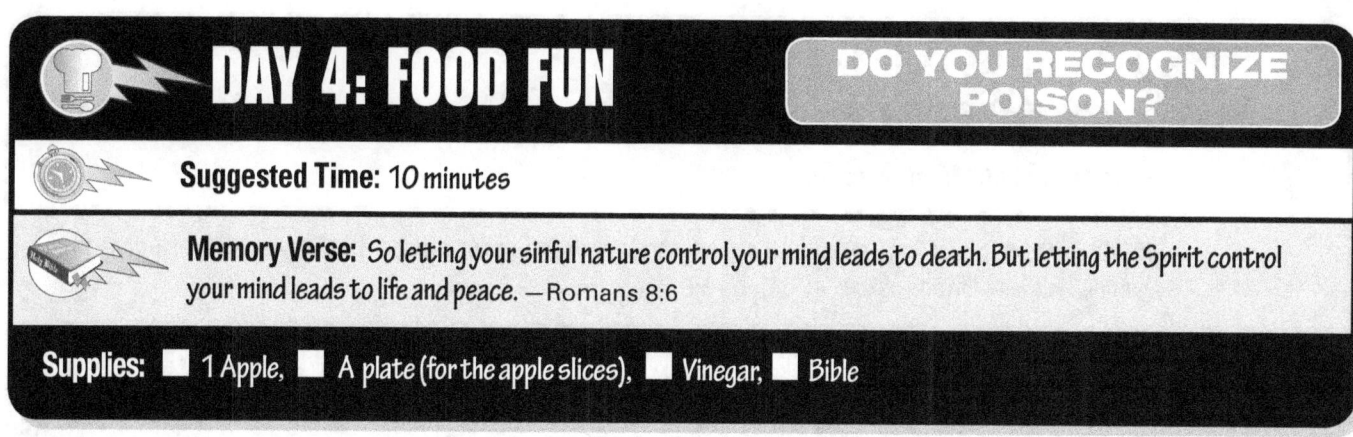

DAY 4: FOOD FUN — DO YOU RECOGNIZE POISON?

Suggested Time: 10 minutes

Memory Verse: So letting your sinful nature control your mind leads to death. But letting the Spirit control your mind leads to life and peace. —Romans 8:6

Supplies: ☐ 1 Apple, ☐ A plate (for the apple slices), ☐ Vinegar, ☐ Bible

Prior to Lesson:

Slice an apple and place a few slices on a plate. Place several drops of vinegar on one slice (enough to make it taste bad) and leave the other slices as they are.

Lesson Instructions:

Who likes apples?

(Let your kids help you. Have each kid choose a slice, and allow them to taste their apples. They will make a sour expression when they taste the "bad apple.")

Who got the good-tasting apple slice? Who picked the sour-tasting slice?

Would you have chosen a different slice if you knew it would taste sour?

Apples are not the only thing that may look good on the outside, but turn out tasting bad on the inside.

Some things look good on the outside, but are bitter once you taste them. *(Display the vinegar.)* Just like this vinegar didn't belong on the apple slice to make it taste sour, there are some things that don't belong on us! Some movies or shows may seem OK at first glance, but they're bitter to our hearts.

How do we learn to tell the good from the bad?

God's Word teaches us the difference between the good and the bad in every situation. Romans 8:6 says, "So letting your sinful nature control your mind leads to death. But letting the Spirit control your mind leads to life and peace." God's thoughts are good thoughts, and the world's thoughts are bad thoughts. Let's say this together, "I choose God's thoughts!"

Variation No. 1: Pickles

Use sweet pickles and dill pickles. Make sure both kinds are similar sizes and see if kids can detect the difference.

Variation No. 2: Sugar Cookies

Make sugar cookies and use sugar crystals or powdered sugar on the tops of the cookies for decoration. On some of the cookies, add alum crystals (available in the spice aisle of your grocery store, near pickling spices) instead of the sugar! It's guaranteed to make your kids pucker without hurting them. You'll make your point very clearly about the sweet and the bitter!

Series: Sweet Life

Home Bible Study for Kids • Week 6: ALL OF MY MIND

DAY 5: GAME TIME — WORMS AWAY!

Suggested Time: 10 minutes

Memory Verse: So letting your sinful nature control your mind leads to death. But letting the Spirit control your mind leads to life and peace. —Romans 8:6

Supplies: ☐ 2 Extra-large cans of pudding (available at bulk grocery stores), ☐ 1 Bag of potting soil, ☐ 20-60 Gelatin-based candies shaped like worms, ☐ 4 Large, clear bowls (available at party stores), ☐ Small trash can, ☐ Upbeat music to play during the game

Prior to Game:

Choose a place outside where the game will be played. Place 2 of the large, clear bowls on the ground and fill them with potting soil. Hide 10 gummy worms in each bowl of potting soil.

Place the other 2 large, clear bowls on the ground a short distance from the bowls with the potting soil, and fill them with pudding. Players will toss their gummy worms to their teammates at the pudding bowls.

Place a small trash can nearby to throw away the sticky pudding worms.

Game Instructions:

Does anyone like worms?

Great! Today, we'll be digging for worms.

Divide into 2 teams with 2 players on each team. Or just have 1 team.

Round 1:

Position 2 players by the bowls containing the worms and the potting soil.

Position the other 2 players next to the pudding bowls, which are located a good tossing distance away.

The players located by the worm bowls will try to find all 10 worms using their hands, and then toss the worms into their teammates' pudding bowls.

Round 2 (option):

Spring a last-minute twist on the kids before the second round begins!

Perform the same game as described in round 1, except have the players near the worm bowls take off their socks and shoes and use their toes to find the worms. The worms will be tossed with hands to teammates at the pudding bowls.

Series: Sweet Life

Rounds 2 and 3 (options):

Consider throwing the old worms away that are sticky with pudding and using new ones, unless there's not a concern for making a mess. The kids will love the added fun of sticky AND dirty worms!

Game Goal:

The team that tosses the most worms into or close to the pudding bowls, wins.

Final Word:

Sometimes wrong thoughts try to invade our minds, just like those worms invaded our yummy pudding. The good news is— God's Word can keep out the worms!

Variation No. 1: Rice and Pennies

Search for pennies in a jar of rice.

Variation No. 2: Rocks and Beans

Dig for rocks or pebbles that you pre-mix with dried beans. The beans can be washed and cooked later and the pebbles tossed.

Notes: _____
_____
_____
_____
_____
_____
_____
_____
_____
_____
_____
_____
_____

Home Bible Study for Kids • Week 6: ALL OF MY MIND

Notes:

Home Bible Study for Kids • Week 6: ALL OF MY MIND

ACTIVITY PAGE — GOOD THOUGHTS CROSSWORD

Memory Verse: So letting your sinful nature control your mind leads to death. But letting the Spirit control your mind leads to life and peace. —Romans 8:6

God desires for His people to fill their minds with things that honor Him. Philippians 4:8-9 says you should "fix your thoughts on what is true, and honorable, and right, and pure, and lovely, and admirable. Think about things that are excellent and worthy of praise. Keep putting into practice all you learned and received from me—everything you heard from me and saw me doing. Then the God of peace will be with you."

As you think about that verse, use the words in it to complete this crossword puzzle. Remember, each word will only fit in one correct way.

TRUE
HONORABLE
RIGHT
PURE
LOVELY
ADMIRABLE
EXCELLENT
WORTHY
PRAISE
PEACE

Series: Sweet Life

Home Bible Study for Kids • Week 6: ALL OF MY MIND

ANSWER KEY

Across

Worthy
Peace
Honorable
Right
Excellent

Down

Admirable
Praise
Pure
True
Lovely

Notes: _____

_____
_____
_____
_____
_____
_____
_____
_____
_____

Series: Sweet Life

WEEK 7: ALL OF MY BODY

 **DAY 1:** BIBLE LESSON—BRAVE YOUNG MEN ▶ PG 100

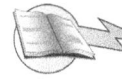 **DAY 2:** READ-ALOUD—B-RAD'S EXCELLENT ADVENTURE, PART 3: "MASTER OF MAKEOVERS" ▶ PG 102

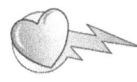 **DAY 3:** GIVING LESSON—THE RIGHT KIND OF "HAND-OUT" ▶ PG 104

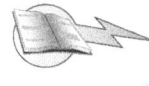 **DAY 4:** OBJECT LESSON—THE MOST EXPENSIVE HOUSE ▶ PG 106

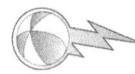 **DAY 5:** GAME TIME—TAKE CARE OF THE TEMPLE ▶ PG 108

 **BONUS:** ACTIVITY PAGE—HEALTHY CHOICES COLORING SHEET ▶ PG 110

 **Memory Verse:** *For God bought you with a high price. So you must honor God with your body.*
—I Corinthians 6:20

Home Bible Study for Kids • Week 7: ALL OF MY BODY

WEEK 7: SNAPSHOT — ALL OF MY BODY

DAY	TYPE OF LESSON	LESSON TITLE	SUPPLIES
Day 1	Bible Lesson	Brave Young Men	None
Day 2	Read-Aloud	B-Rad's Excellent Adventure, Part 3: "Master of Makeovers"	None
Day 3	Giving Lesson	The Right Kind of "Hand-Out"	1-2 Cups flour in a quart-sized bag, Gardening gloves, A baseball mitt, A small amount of chocolate syrup
Day 4	Object Lesson	The Most Expensive House	Pictures of expensive, beautiful homes or have open a real-estate website with pictures the kids can look at, A picture of each child
Day 5	Game Time	Take Care of the Temple	Create a makeshift tub: a laundry basket or small child's pool or box large enough for a kid to sit in, A shower cap and bath brush, A container to fill with unpeeled bananas cut in half, Masking tape, A stopwatch or timekeeper, Upbeat music
Bonus	Activity Page	Healthy Choices Coloring Sheet	1 Copy for each child

Lesson Introduction:

In a society where so many people mistreat their bodies, we should let our children know that our bodies belong to us in one sense, but they are also God's dwelling place—the Holy Spirit dwells in us. It is our love for God that will bring the desire to honor Him in our decisions about our bodies. He cannot fully function through a dysfunctional, broken-down home. As you reinforce how much God loves your kids, you will lead them to make decisions based on their love for Him. Remember, we love Him because He loved us first!

Commander Dana
—Commander Dana

Lesson Outline:

Train your children that, like everything else in their lives, their bodies belong to the Lord. For this reason, they should take care of their bodies by respecting, caring for, exercising and feeding them with healthy food. God has a plan for each Superkid, and part of being ready for that plan is being physically ready to do anything and everything the Holy Spirit instructs them to do.

I. YOUR BODY IS A HOUSE 1 Corinthians 6:19

a. God's Word calls our bodies the temple of the Holy Spirit.

b. Temples are places that get special care and respect.

c. Many people today mistreat and disrespect their bodies.

d. God made a wonderful design when He made our bodies!

II. YOUR HOUSE WAS VERY EXPENSIVE 1 Corinthians 6:20

a. God paid the highest price for your temple.

b. A valuable house should get the best treatment.

c. Jesus' blood is the price tag for our "house." Our heavenly Father definitely lives in the most expensive house, ever!

III. GOD CHOSE YOUR HOUSE TO LIVE IN

a. Our Father could have chosen to live anywhere. Acts 7:7-48

b. We clean our natural house when a guest is coming to visit.

c. What kind of house are you letting God live in?

Let's look at it like this: God lets us decide how clean and nice His "house" will be. It's up to us.

Will you try and keep your temple in great shape for God?

Can you think of ways to improve your temple?

What are some tips you could give a younger friend on maintaining God's temple?

Home Bible Study for Kids • Week 7: ALL OF MY BODY

DAY 1: BIBLE LESSON — BRAVE YOUNG MEN

Memory Verse: *For God bought you with a high price. So you must honor God with your body.*
—I Corinthians 6:20

This week, you'll be teaching your kids about God's desire for us to present our bodies as a sacrifice to Him. A great example of God honoring that sacrifice is in the story of four brave, young men who followed God's laws over man's laws. God blessed their decision. There were a lot of rules for God's people under the old covenant. Thankfully, under the new covenant, we do not have the same list of rules to follow because Jesus came and fulfilled the law with His sacrifice. And yet, God still blesses those who honor their "temple."

Read Daniel 1:8-20:

But Daniel was determined not to defile himself by eating the food and wine given to them by the king. He asked the chief of staff for permission not to eat these unacceptable foods. Now God had given the chief of staff both respect and affection for Daniel. But he responded, "I am afraid of my lord the king, who has ordered that you eat this food and wine. If you become pale and thin compared to the other youths your age, I am afraid the king will have me beheaded."

Daniel spoke with the attendant who had been appointed by the chief of staff to look after Daniel, Hananiah, Mishael, and Azariah. "Please test us for ten days on a diet of vegetables and water," Daniel said. "At the end of the ten days, see how we look compared to the other young men who are eating the king's food. Then make your decision in light of what you see." The attendant agreed to Daniel's suggestion and tested them for ten days.

At the end of the ten days, Daniel and his three friends looked healthier and better nourished than the young men who had been eating the food assigned by the king. So after that, the attendant fed them only vegetables instead of the food and wine provided for the others.

God gave these four young men an unusual aptitude for understanding every aspect of literature and wisdom. And God gave Daniel the special ability to interpret the meanings of visions and dreams.

When the training period ordered by the king was completed, the chief of staff brought all the young men to King Nebuchadnezzar. The king talked with them, and no one impressed him as much as Daniel, Hananiah, Mishael, and Azariah [Shadrach, Meshach, and Abednego]. So they entered the royal service. Whenever the king consulted them in any matter requiring wisdom and balanced judgment, he found them ten times more capable than any of the magicians and enchanters in his entire kingdom.

Discussion Questions:

1. **What did the four Hebrews do differently from all the other captives?**
   They requested not to eat foods that would go against God's laws.

2. **What was the official's response to this request?**
   He was afraid that he would get into trouble, but the guard he placed in charge of the young men agreed to Daniel's request.

Series: Sweet Life

3. What happened after the trial period of 10 days?
Daniel and his friends were stronger and looked better than all the other captives.

4. What did King Nebuchadnezzar do?
He talked with the four young men and found they were smarter and better than all his enchanters and magicians.

5. What does this teach us?
God honored Daniel and his friends because they kept His commandments. Although we are not required to eat only vegetables and have a rigid diet as they did, God does ask us to "sacrifice" our bodies. That means we should eat healthy foods, get plenty of exercise, and take good care of these amazing temples that He has blessed us with. Intentionally taking care of our bodies is pleasing to God.

Variation: Healthy Bites

This week, as you teach this lesson, consider introducing your children to some healthy foods that they may have never tried before or usually avoid. It's a great opportunity to let them put into practice what they're learning!

Notes: _____

Home Bible Study for Kids • Week 7: ALL OF MY BODY

DAY 2: READ-ALOUD — B-RAD'S EXCELLENT ADVENTURE, PART 3: "MASTER OF MAKEOVERS"

Suggested Time: 15 minutes

Memory Verse: For God bought you with a high price. So you must honor God with your body.
—I Corinthians 6:20

Background: This week continues the five-week read-aloud series, "All of Me," about a writer's discussions of his developing story with his younger friend Tyson, a surfer with a dry sense of humor, who's slightly sarcastic, but all in fun. At the end of this five-week series, the audience will discover that the "Writer" is really B-Rad himself. This story is loosely based on the life of the Apostle Paul. This story includes fun surfing lingo. The unusual terms are defined in parentheses.

Story:

The writer sat placidly, under his shady umbrella beside the shore, his pencil poised above his writing pad, looking out across the crashing waves for inspiration for the next section in his story. Abruptly, he was interrupted by his friend Tyson.

"Hey, what's crackin', dude?" Tyson began.

"The same thing that was crackin' the last two times I saw you, dude."

Tyson responded with a laugh, "Rad. So is your story finished?"

The writer paused, pencil in midair. "If I could just get the fans to stop interrupting me, I'd be much further along, but certain surfers keep pestering me for the next part of the adventure. By the way, dude, are you riding the waves today?"

Tyson chuckled at the obvious reference to himself. "Of course I'm here to ride the waves, man! But I'll wait if you need to run the latest chapter past a captive, er, captivated audience."

"Hmmm...let's see...I'm not sure if I remember where I left off," he mumbled, scrambling through his notebook.

Tyson piped up, "Well, Brad met Andy at The Coffee Shack. After several conversations over iced mochas, Brad began thinking maybe God wanted him to be a witness to the surfers who came in for a treat from breaking the waves. So, Andy offered to tutor him in surfer lingo and skills, so unsaved surfers would actually listen to what he had to say and respect him for their common interest."

The writer, obviously flattered by Tyson's intrigue with his story, stopped flipping through his notebook and laughed. "Hey, you *were* listening to my story and not just humoring me, weren't you?"

Tyson grinned, "I'll admit, it's a pretty good beginning. I mean, it's totally rad that Andy is teaching Brad the lingo and all, but there's no beach in the world where a surfer's gonna get amped (excited) over some bookworm guy who's never joined in an all skate (where someone is riding a really long wave and calls, 'All skate!' for many boarders to join in the ride) or experienced an airdrop (a very late takeoff where the surfer drops through the air to the bottom of the wave). Any surfer worth his salt will know that Brad's a Barney (a beginner)!"

"Exactly! That's why Andy is introducing Brad to Les," the writer said. "Les promises that he's the king of 'island makeovers' and can make sure no one dubs Brad as a chrubee (a wanna-be surfer). Les has worked on tough cases and knows how to get the surfer look down pat. In fact, by the time Les gets done with Brad, he's so cool, everyone calls him B-Rad.

Series: Sweet Life

Home Bible Study for Kids • Week 7: ALL OF MY BODY

"Of course, the next problem is that B-Rad talked and looked like a surfer, but had one gnarly snag: He couldn't surf or ride a *baby wave,* much less hang with the big Kahuna (those who surf with skill)."

Tyson looked puzzled. "But everyone is going to know Les has just made an accessory man (someone who wears the clothes but doesn't ride the surf). I mean, no one's gonna listen to him talking about Jesus, especially not a real surfer."

The writer nodded. "Right on! B-Rad has got to get in shape. The longest exercise he gets is walking from the bus to his classroom."

Tyson chuckled. "The men in grey suits (sharks) will devour him if he's not in shape. So how long does it take him to learn to surf?"

"A week," replied the writer.

"Impossible!" Tyson responded. "Dude, even if your story *is* fiction, you should make it realistic. It took me a year to learn and three years before I moved out of the random stander (inexperienced surfer) club."

"Well, bro, you're right. It sounds weird, but that's the way the surf's rollin' in this story," the writer said. "God helped B-Rad become a good surfer so he could lead others to Christ through his example."

Tyson paused. "OK, I'll give you that. But he's gotta be real if he's gonna hang ten in the surfing world."

"With God, anything is possible, right?"

"Sure, if you say so. Soooo, did B-Rad start preaching to the surfers, or what?"

Thoughtfully, the writer responded, "Not quite. He needs some help from other Christian surfers if B-Rad is going to make some waves. It's not going to be easy. He used to be the surfers' enemy, and he's going to have to earn their trust, convincing them that he's real and that he's changed."

"Come on, man. How's he s'posed to do that?"

The writer chuckled as he picked up his pencil and turned to a clean sheet of paper. "You're asking for the next chapter. Get out and ride some waves so I can get it on paper. Later, dude."

TO BE CONTINUED NEXT WEEK…

Discussion Questions:

Use these questions as conversation starters. Enjoy this time of heart-to-heart conversation with your children.

1. Why was it important for B-Rad to know how to surf?

2. Can God use our physical bodies to witness to people? Can you give some examples?

3. Does God ever call us to learn something new or use one of our existing talents to reach people for Jesus?

4. What talents do you have that God may be able to use?

Notes:_____
_____
_____

Series: Sweet Life

Home Bible Study for Kids • Week 7: ALL OF MY BODY

DAY 3: GIVING LESSON — THE RIGHT KIND OF "HAND-OUT"

Suggested Time: 10 minutes

Offering Scripture: Generous hands are blessed hands because they give bread to the poor. —Proverbs 22:9 MSG

Supplies: ☐ 1-2 Cups flour in a quart-sized bag, ☐ Gardening gloves, ☐ A baseball mitt, ☐ A small amount of chocolate syrup (to appear like automotive grease)

Lesson Instructions:

We have a little test today, but before we get started, I'll need helpers. *(If four helpers are not available, have two people switch parts.)*

The first person places the gardening gloves on his/her hands.

The second person places the baseball mitt on his/her hand.

The third person covers his/her hands with flour.

The fourth person covers his/her hands with the "automotive grease."

(Have each kid display the item or substance on their hands, one by one, and allow kids to discuss what kind of work their hands might perform. Have the "baker" (the one with flour on his/her hands) and the "mechanic" (the one with chocolate syrup on his/her hands) wash hands before you continue the lesson.)

Was it hard to figure out what kind of work each person's hands could perform?

The "baker's hands" could be hands that love to bake something special and yummy for their family. The "baseball player's hands" could belong to someone who loves to be outside and has fun playing with friends. The "mechanic's hands" could be hands that like to take things apart and put them back together. And the "gardener's hands" might belong to someone who enjoys making things look and smell beautiful!

Kids, it's awesome when people use their hands in ways that please God. In fact, there's a scripture that teaches us about a special type of hands that do just that. Proverbs 22:9, MSG says, "Generous hands are blessed hands because they give bread to the poor."

What kind of "hands" is this verse talking about?

Generous hands are hands that are not stingy, but always open and ready to give.

God's Word says that generous hands are blessed, and when our hands are blessed, it means we always have plenty to give to others.

Let's keep a close watch on our hands and make sure they are hands that please God. When we do that, we know that whatever our hands do will always be blessed!

Series: Sweet Life

Variation No. 1: One Child

If your group is small, even one child can be your "volunteer" for each job to demonstrate separately what types of hands are useful.

Variation No. 2: Helping Hands

Think of a way to be "helping hands" this week. What is on your children's hearts to do for someone they know with a specific need? Practical application really is the best!

Notes: _____

_____
_____
_____
_____
_____
_____
_____
_____
_____
_____
_____
_____
_____
_____
_____
_____
_____
_____
_____
_____
_____

Home Bible Study for Kids • Week 7: ALL OF MY BODY

DAY 4: OBJECT LESSON — THE MOST EXPENSIVE HOUSE

Suggested Time: 10 minutes

Memory Verse: For God bought you with a high price. So you must honor God with your body.
—I Corinthians 6:20

Supplies:
- ☐ Pictures of expensive, beautiful homes or have open a real-estate website with pictures the kids can look at
- ☐ A picture of each child

Prior to Lesson:

Place the pictures face down on a table.

Lesson Instructions:

How many of you have ever seen a really big, beautiful house? *(Have your kids describe what they saw.)*

A house like that can be very expensive.

Can anyone think of some reasons these homes cost a lot of money?

Possible answers:

Beautiful homes require a lot of work/labor.

Beautiful homes often contain expensive materials.

The architectural designs are expensive.

Beautiful homes require a lot of maintenance.

(Turn the pictures of the beautiful homes over and allow the kids to see them, as each one is being discussed.)

The first two pictures are both beautiful homes that someone built. People saw the homes and thought, *That would be the perfect place for me to live!* Then, they paid whatever that house cost so they could live there. Now, the best house...

(Display the picture of each child.)

This house is special. You may not think that you are a "house," but God certainly does. Our heavenly Father could live anywhere, on any planet or place, but He decided that you are the "house" He wants to live in.

God thought and planned for each of you before you were born. Then, God our Father sent Jesus to pay the highest price for you. He gave the best He had so you could be the perfect "house" to live in (1 Corinthians 6:20).

But He won't just barge in. He'll wait until He's invited to move in!

If anyone ever asks you about the most expensive and beautiful house in the world, you can tell them to read 1 Corinthians 6:20. You are the best "house" God ever built!

Series: Sweet Life

Variation: Internet

Use a real-estate website on the Internet instead of actual photos. Allow the kids to determine the actual price range you want to search for "dream homes." They can choose the number of bathrooms, bedrooms, acreage and different amenities they might define as amazing.

Notes: _____
_____
_____
_____
_____
_____
_____
_____
_____
_____
_____
_____
_____
_____
_____
_____
_____
_____
_____
_____
_____
_____
_____
_____
_____
_____
_____

Home Bible Study for Kids • Week 7: ALL OF MY BODY

DAY 5: GAME TIME — TAKE CARE OF THE TEMPLE

Suggested Time: 10 minutes

Memory Verse: For God bought you with a high price. So you must honor God with your body.
—I Corinthians 6:20

Supplies: ☐ Create a makeshift tub: a laundry basket, small child's pool or box large enough for a kid to sit in, ☐ A shower cap and bath brush, ☐ A container to fill with unpeeled bananas cut in half, ☐ Masking tape, ☐ A stopwatch or timekeeper, ☐ Upbeat music to play during game

Prior to Game:

Create 3 stations:

Station 1 will be the "bathtub" station. Place the "tub," shower cap and bath brush where everyone in the room can see.

Station 2 will be the "gym" station. This area can be a taped-out square on the floor.

Station 3 will be the "banana-eating" station.

Game Instructions:

At station 1, each player will place a shower cap on their head and step into the "tub" and pretend to scrub their back 5 times with the bath brush.

Next, the player will run to the "gym" station, and perform 5 jumping jacks.

Finally, station 3 is meal time! Each player will run to the assistant holding the container filled with banana halves, take a banana, peel and eat it completely.

Using the stopwatch, keep track of which player "cares for their temple" the fastest.

Game Goal:

This game is designed to help kids recognize the importance of honoring God by taking care of their bodies. After all, they are His temple!

Final Word:

This is a perfect opportunity to remind kids that God is trusting them to take good care of His house, their bodies.

Mention to them that God desires for His house to receive the best care! Let's honor God by keeping His house in top shape! Some of the practical ways we do that is with healthy, well-rounded diets, good amounts of sleep, enough exercise and guarding what goes into our minds and hearts. What are some areas they would like to improve?

Series: Sweet Life

Variation: Snack Attack

Be sure to choose a food that's a favorite with your children. If kids really don't enjoy bananas, choose another healthy snack they love like carrot sticks, peanut butter on whole-grain crackers, or mini-boxes of raisins!

Notes: _____
_____
_____
_____
_____
_____
_____
_____
_____
_____
_____
_____
_____
_____
_____
_____
_____
_____
_____
_____
_____
_____
_____
_____
_____

Home Bible Study for Kids • Week 7: ALL OF MY BODY

ACTIVITY PAGE

HEALTHY CHOICES COLORING SHEET

Memory Verse: For God bought you with a high price. So you must honor God with your body.
—I Corinthians 6:20

Everyone must decide how to honor God with his/her body in the best possible way. We must each decide which foods to eat and which to avoid, or to only eat occasionally. The table below is filled with many foods, but only some are really nourishing for your body. After you color the picture, circle the foods that are healthy and should be eaten often.

HEALTHY CHOICES

Series: Sweet Life

WEEK 8: ALL OF MY PAST

- **DAY 1: BIBLE LESSON—THE SAMARITAN WOMAN** ▸ PG 114
- **DAY 2: READ-ALOUD—B-RAD'S EXCELLENT ADVENTURE, PART 4: "WICKED PAST"** ▸ PG 116
- **DAY 3: GIVING LESSON—GOD'S HALL OF FAME** ▸ PG 118
- **DAY 4: ACADEMY LAB—BLOWN AWAY** ▸ PG 120
- **DAY 5: GAME TIME—TOSS THE PAST** ▸ PG 122
- **BONUS: ACTIVITY PAGE—LIVING WATER PUZZLE** ▸ PG 124

Memory Verse: But I focus on this one thing: Forgetting the past and looking forward to what lies ahead. —Philippians 3:13

Home Bible Study for Kids • Week 8: ALL OF MY PAST

WEEK 8: SNAPSHOT — ALL OF MY PAST

DAY	TYPE OF LESSON	LESSON TITLE	SUPPLIES
Day 1	Bible Lesson	The Samaritan Woman	None
Day 2	Read-Aloud	B-Rad's Excellent Adventure, Part 4: "Wicked Past"	None
Day 3	Giving Lesson	God's Hall of Fame	Mr. Potato Head® game (with the Mr. Potato Head® parts)
Day 4	Academy Lab	Blown Away	6-Ounce yogurt container or small-sized sour cream container (cleaned), Scissors and knife, Medium-sized balloon, Rubber band, 18 6-8-Ounce paper cups
Day 5	Game Time	Toss the Past	2 Cartons hard-boiled eggs (or plastic Easter eggs or wads of paper to substitute for eggs), 1 Large plastic tarp, 2 Trash cans (or 1 per team), Upbeat music
Bonus	Activity Page	Living Water Puzzle	1 Copy for each child

Lesson Introduction:

Children are often exposed to some very tough situations. The enemy will try to hold them back with memories that confuse and torment. These memories can be a yoke and a burden, weighing them down and keeping them stuck. The world's remedy is self-pity.

Even if your children are not struggling with challenging memories, they will meet other kids who have very difficult circumstances to process. It's a great opportunity to learn that God's remedy is His love and His Word! The Anointing of God will destroy those yokes and lift the burden of grief and remorse right off those kids, permanently!

Your part is to preach the good news that there is a bright future in God, and that no bad thing can keep it from them. They need to reach for something! Of course, God has plenty for them to reach for, but you need to lay out some attainable goals for them, as well. Put your thinking cap on, and get creative. Think like God for a minute. You'll come up with something!

Commander Dana
—Commander Dana

Home Bible Study for Kids • Week 8: ALL OF MY PAST

Lesson Outline:

Your children, like all other Christians, are not defined by their past mistakes or unhappy incidents. Those sins and memories are under the blood of Jesus. As you teach this lesson, encourage your children to embrace the freedom they have in Christ. God loves them, Jesus died for them and they are free!

I. OUR MEMORIES WERE CREATED BY GOD

    a. Our minds were made to help us remember things.

    b. They were designed to hold good memories.

    c. Bad memories started in the Garden of Eden. Genesis 3:24

II. SOME THINGS NEED TO BE FORGOTTEN

    a. Ungodly things we have seen or heard.

    c. Bad things that have happened to us.

    d. Even mistakes we have made—God forgets about our mistakes! Hebrews 8:12; Isaiah 43:25

III. REACH FOR THE PRIZE

    a. Some people think about the past all the time.

    b. Paul said it's important to forget our negative past. Philippians 3:13

    c. To reach the prize God has for you, don't look back!

    d. It is impossible to run your best race if you are looking behind you. Looking ahead means looking at the bright future our heavenly Father has planned out for us.

Notes:_____

_____

_____

_____

_____

_____

_____

_____

Series: Sweet Life

Home Bible Study for Kids • Week 8: ALL OF MY PAST

DAY 1: BIBLE LESSON — THE SAMARITAN WOMAN

Memory Verse: But I focus on this one thing: Forgetting the past and looking forward to what lies ahead.
—Philippians 3:13

This week's Bible story contains a wonderful message of forgiveness. As you teach this lesson, let the Holy Spirit lead your family in discovering any areas where your children need to receive or extend forgiveness. Enjoy watching Him work in your family this week and discover the power of forgiveness!

Read John 4:7-26, 28-30:

Soon a Samaritan woman came to draw water, and Jesus said to her, "Please give me a drink." He was alone at the time because his disciples had gone into the village to buy some food.

The woman was surprised, for Jews refuse to have anything to do with Samaritans. She said to Jesus, "You are a Jew, and I am a Samaritan woman. Why are you asking me for a drink?"

Jesus replied, "If you only knew the gift God has for you and who you are speaking to, you would ask me, and I would give you living water."

"But sir, you don't have a rope or a bucket," she said, "and this well is very deep. Where would you get this living water? And besides, do you think you're greater than our ancestor Jacob, who gave us this well? How can you offer better water than he and his sons and his animals enjoyed?"

Jesus replied, "Anyone who drinks this water will soon become thirsty again. But those who drink the water I give will never be thirsty again. It becomes a fresh, bubbling spring within them, giving them eternal life."

"Please, sir," the woman said, "give me this water! Then I'll never be thirsty again, and I won't have to come here to get water."

"Go and get your husband," Jesus told her.

"I don't have a husband," the woman replied.

Jesus said, "You're right! You don't have a husband—for you have had five husbands, and you aren't even married to the man you're living with now. You certainly spoke the truth!"

"Sir," the woman said, "you must be a prophet. So tell me, why is it that you Jews insist that Jerusalem is the only place of worship, while we Samaritans claim it is here at Mount Gerizim, where our ancestors worshiped?"

Jesus replied, "Believe me, dear woman, the time is coming when it will no longer matter whether you worship the Father on this mountain or in Jerusalem. You Samaritans know very little about the one you worship, while we Jews know all about him, for salvation comes through the Jews. But the time is coming—indeed it's here now—when true worshipers will worship the Father in spirit and in truth. The Father is looking for those who will worship him that way. For God is Spirit, so those who worship him must worship in spirit and in truth."

The woman said, "I know the Messiah is coming—the one who is called Christ. When he comes, he will explain everything to us."

Series: Sweet Life

Then Jesus told her, "I am the Messiah!"

The woman left her water jar beside the well and ran back to the village, telling everyone, "Come and see a man who told me everything I ever did! Could he possibly be the Messiah?" So the people came streaming from the village to see him.

Discussion Questions:

1. **What did Jesus ask the lady to do for Him?**
   He asked her for a drink of water from the well.

2. **Why did she think this was strange and unusual?**
   They were from two different people groups: Jews and Samaritans. The two groups were notorious for their prejudices against each other.

3. **What did Jesus say to her response that they were from different groups?**
   He said that she would be asking Him for a drink if she only knew who He was.

4. **Did she understand what He meant?**
   No, she thought they were still talking about water, but Jesus was talking about eternal life and forgiveness.

5. **What did the woman say when Jesus told her to call her husband?**
   She said she didn't have one.

6. **What caused the woman to think that Jesus was the Messiah?**
   He told her all that she had done and yet continued to have a conversation with her. He was not judging her, but telling her who He was and that He had come to give her "living water" so that she would thirst no more!

7. **What do you think God wants to teach us from this passage?**
   God wants us to know that He has come to forgive sins, no matter what we have done! He wants to give us eternal, living water through His Son, Jesus!

Notes: _____
_____
_____
_____
_____
_____
_____
_____
_____
_____
_____
_____

Home Bible Study for Kids • Week 8: ALL OF MY PAST

DAY 2: READ-ALOUD — B-RAD'S EXCELLENT ADVENTURE, PART 4: "WICKED PAST"

 **Suggested Time:** 15 minutes

 **Memory Verse:** But I focus on this one thing: Forgetting the past and looking forward to what lies ahead.
—Philippians 3:13

 **Background:** This week continues the five-week read-aloud series, "All of Me," about a writer's discussions of his developing story with his younger friend Tyson, a surfer with a dry sense of humor, who's slightly sarcastic, but all in fun. At the end of this five-week series, the audience will discover that the "Writer" is really B-Rad himself. This story is loosely based on the life of the Apostle Paul. This story includes fun surfing lingo. The unusual terms are defined in parentheses.

Story:

Tyson joins his friend, the writer, who appears to be lounging in a chair under a large beach umbrella, sipping a cola and staring out at the waves from the sandy beach. "Dude, are you becoming a beach bum or what? Last time I saw you, you were in the exact same position, except you actually were moving a pencil in that frazzled notebook of yours!"

Laughing, the writer looks up. "Aren't you supposed to say 'What's crackin'?' before you beg for the next episode of my book? Besides, I thought having a good chillax (relaxing time on the beach) was good for the soul!"

Tyson flops down in the sand with his surfboard beside the writer. "Come on, dude. You're boss (cool, awesome). Tell me what's crackin' with B-Rad in your story. No bogus parts. Shoot it straight. Is B-Rad successful in breaking waves and sharing the news? You said he needed help from other Christian surfers if he wanted to break some waves."

"Sure, that's right. But that's not going to be easy, since B-Rad used to be one of their biggest enemies. It could be tough to get their trust and convince them he's really changed," the writer responded.

Tyson smiled, "Sure, I can relate to that one!"

With a flip of his notebook, the writer found the spot where they'd left off previously in the story. "So, Andy introduces B-Rad to Blaine. He's a crusher (a guy who surfs hard) and da bomb (the greatest). Blaine is also part of a Christian surfer group called the RAD surfers."

Tyson interrupted, "Won't Blaine be suspicious that B-Rad is trying to trick his dudes? I mean, one day he's lying to the police ratting them out for things they didn't do and then he's claiming he's a saved surfing machine? It doesn't jive for me."

"Sure, you're right, but B-Rad has done a lot worse than just lie about the RAD surfers. The story goes that before B-Rad became a follower of Jesus, he met a RAD surfer named Jody. They were hanging for a bit, but then Jody started talking about Jesus, which totally infuriated B-Rad. So he thought he'd shut Jody up for a bit. He broke into the RAD surf shack and broke Jody's surfboard."

Tyson interjected, "LAME-O, dude! Totally un-cool. What was he thinking?"

The writer continued, "The next day, Jody went out to ride some waves without realizing his rudder was damaged. He started out vigorously, ready to lacerate (slice and ride) a wave and then he was gone."

"Gone? Whaddya mean 'gone'? As in shark bait? Left town? Come on, man. Don't go there with your story!"

Series: Sweet Life

"I'm just tellin' you like it's written, dude," the writer continued without a glance at his notebook. "Jody entered a choppy barrel by himself, but never rode out. His body was never recovered."

With an engrossed sigh, Tyson stood. "Dude, I did not see that coming in your story. You got me. I thought Jody and B-Rad were going to become friends and be cruisin' around town together or hanging at lunch together. There's no way the RAD surfers are going to bring him in to their tight group now."

Tyson paced a few steps to the water's edge, dipping his toes into the cool, ocean water. He paused and looked out at the beauty of the waves crashing into the sea. Then he walked back over to his friend expectantly. "So, what's next for B-Rad? Do the cops put him away? Do the RAD surfers find out and turn him in? I gotta hand it to you. You've got me coming back for the rest of the story, dude! Wouldn't that be murder or something like that?"

"Well, first of all, Blaine watched B-Rad and was convinced that he was for real, even though he knew about his past. B-Rad shared about Jesus and how his life had changed because of the seeds Jody had planted in his heart with all their conversations about Jesus. The RAD surfers were convinced that he was solid."

"I bet that took longer than a week," Tyson spoke ruefully.

"True. It wasn't easy. But B-Rad shared his mission of how he wanted to win over the BAD surfers. They called themselves that as an acronym for "Bullies Against Disciples."

"Trippin'!" Tyson interjected.

"Yep. They're gnarly, bad dudes, but B-Rad wanted to make a connection with them and the RAD surfers were his ticket to understanding the surfing culture better."

"Crazy!"

"Maybe so, but crazy with God's power is OK, ya know?" replied the writer.

"And then?" asked Tyson.

"Well, I need to work on that part," the writer responded, flipping to another clean sheet of paper.

"OK, I'll let you get to it. I need to go break some waves anyway." Tyson ran off, board in hand.

TO BE CONTINUED NEXT WEEK…

Discussion Questions:

Use these questions as conversation starters. Enjoy this time of heart-to-heart conversation with your children.

1. Do you believe that Jesus can make a big change in a person's life, in the way they think and act? Why?

2. How has Jesus changed your life?

3. Are you defined by what you were like before Christ? Why or why not?

4. Parents, share your testimony with your children. What difference has Jesus made in your life?

Variation: Journaling

Have your older children write their salvation testimony. Have them include any changes that have happened thanks to their new life in Christ.

Home Bible Study for Kids • Week 8: ALL OF MY PAST

DAY 3: GIVING LESSON — GOD'S HALL OF FAME

Suggested Time: 10 minutes

Offering Scripture: Enter his gates with thanksgiving and a thank offering and into His courts with praise! Be thankful and say so to Him, bless and affectionately praise His name! —Psalm 100:4 AMP

Supplies: ☐ Mr. Potato Head® (with the Mr. Potato Head® parts)

Lesson Instructions:

Have you seen Mr. Potato Head®? Have you ever played with one?

Mr. Potato Head® is a lot of fun. You may think he was created after the movie Toy Story®, but he's actually been around much longer.

Can you guess when Mr. Potato Head® was created?

Well, he's been around since the 1950s, a lot longer than most superhero characters. Here are some interesting facts about him:

- April 30, 1952, Mr. Potato Head® was the first toy ever advertised on television.
- Over 1 million were sold during the first year of production.
- There have been many other Mr. Potato Heads® added to the family. Have you seen any? (Mr. and Mrs. Potato Head®, Mr. Potato Head Sporty®, Mr. Potato Head Darth Vader® and Mr. Potato Head Spider-Spud® are just a few, as well as suitcases with accessories for your spudly family).
- In 2000, Mr. Potato Head® was inducted into the Toy Hall of Fame®.

How does a toy get inducted into the Toy Hall of Fame®? Let me tell you what it takes for a toy to even be considered.

- Icon status: The toy must be widely recognized, respected and remembered.
- Longevity: The toy cannot be a passing fad, but has been popular over several generations.
- Discovery: The toy fosters learning, creativity or discovery, through play.
- Innovation: The toy has profoundly changed play or toy design. A toy may be inducted into the Toy Hall of Fame® on the basis of this criterion alone, without having met all of the first three.[1]

(Take Mr. Potato Head® out of the package and lay out all the parts. Begin telling the kids they were created a long time ago too — but by our loving heavenly Father God.)

Are you thankful for all the toys that were created for you to have fun with?

- No wonder the "Spud Man" has been around so long. I had fun talking about Mr. Potato Head® and putting his ears, arms, feet, mouth and eyes together. God put you together in a so much better way—His perfect creation way—so all your parts could offer praise to Him!

---

[1] www.toyhalloffame.org/nominate

Series: Sweet Life

Let's read Psalm 100:4 together: "Enter into His gates with thanksgiving and a thank offering and into His courts with praise! Be thankful and say so to Him, bless and affectionately praise His name!"

It took almost 50 years for Mr. Potato Head® to get into the Toy Hall of Fame®. But, you have free access, whenever you'd like, to come running into God's gates with thanksgiving and a thank offering, and into His courts with praise!

You can trust Him with all you have. As you give your offering, let your Creator know how thankful and ready you are to enter HIS HALL OF FAME!

Notes: _____
_____
_____
_____
_____
_____
_____
_____
_____
_____
_____
_____
_____
_____
_____
_____
_____
_____
_____
_____
_____
_____
_____
_____

Home Bible Study for Kids • Week 8: ALL OF MY PAST

DAY 4: ACADEMY LAB — BLOWN AWAY

Suggested Time: 10 minutes

Memory Verse: But I focus on this one thing: Forgetting the past and looking forward to what lies ahead.
—Philippians 3:13

Supplies: ☐ 6-Ounce yogurt container or small-sized sour cream container (cleaned): Label the yogurt container with the words "FORGET THE PAST," ☐ Scissors and knife, ☐ Medium-sized balloon, ☐ Rubber band, ☐ 18 6-8-Ounce paper cups (6 per tower): One tower labeled "Bad Things I've Heard," one tower labeled "Bad Things I've Seen," and one tower labeled "My Mistakes"

Experiment:

1. Cut a small hole in the bottom of the yogurt or sour cream container. The hole should be approximately 1/2 inch in diameter. Prep this container and label your cup stacks prior to the lesson. The remainder of the experiment can be performed during your lesson time.

2. Cut the rolled edge off the mouth of the balloon and stretch the balloon across the top opening of the container. Secure the balloon to the top edge of the container with a rubber band.

3. Tap on the balloon to produce a small burst of air out the hole in the bottom of the container. This will be the "air cannon."

4. On a table, build the three cup stacks using the six cups labeled for each tower. Stack each tower pyramid-style with three cups forming the bottom row, two cups forming the middle row, and place the last cup on the top with the tower name facing the kids.

One pyramid will be the "Bad Things I've Heard" tower. The next will be the "Bad Things I've Seen" tower, and the third will be the "My Mistakes" tower. The air cannon will be used to knock over the "cup towers" as the lesson is taught. *(Feel free at any time to have a kid help with this!)*

Lesson Instructions:

Wouldn't it be great if we could knock out our past with an air cannon? Today, I'm going to show you how to make one.

(Construct the air cannon and explain the process as you are doing it.)

Now that my air cannon is put together, I can show you what the Lord thinks about our past and how He wants us to handle things that have happened that aren't good.

These towers represent three negative areas in our lives that can hold us back, if we let them. *(Build each tower as you talk about that area.)*

Have you ever heard bad things that got stuck in your mind and wouldn't go away?

Check out my first tower. I call this one "Bad Things I've Heard."

Series: Sweet Life

In Philippians 3:13, the Word says to forget the past and look forward to what lies ahead. When you do, bad things will be blown out of the way as you obey.

(Use the air cannon to blow down the tower!)

Sometimes, things you see can be even more difficult to forget than things you hear. Images on TV, the Internet or things you've seen people do can seem impossible to get rid of. But God's Word works on those too! Forget the past and look forward to what lies ahead! *(Knock down tower 2!)*

Last, but not least, we are going to blow away our third tower, "My Mistakes." Everybody has made mistakes; but when you repent, God forgives you. He doesn't remember it anymore and He doesn't want us to let the memory of our mistakes stay around either!

So, what should we do with the tower of "My Mistakes"?

Right! Let's blow it out of here! Say it with me, "I forget the past and look forward to what lies ahead!" *(Blow away tower 3!)*

Never forget that letting the bad things you've heard or seen, or mistakes you've made, stay in your memory can build a fortress to keep you from looking forward to all the good plans God has for your future. So, the next time negative thoughts show up, think of our "FORGET THE PAST" air cannon, and blow them away!

Notes: _____
_____
_____
_____
_____
_____
_____
_____
_____
_____
_____
_____
_____
_____
_____
_____
_____
_____
_____

DAY 5: GAME TIME — TOSS THE PAST

Suggested Time: 8-10 minutes

Memory Verse: But I focus on this one thing: Forgetting the past and looking forward to what lies ahead.
—Philippians 3:13

Supplies: ☐ 2 Cartons hard-boiled eggs (or plastic Easter eggs or wads of paper to substitute for eggs), ☐ 1 Large plastic tarp, ☐ 2 Trash cans (or 1 per team), ☐ Upbeat music to play during game

Prior to Game:

Prepare two cartons of hard-boiled eggs (one carton of eggs per team, so depending on the number of people participating, the number of eggs may be modified).

Choose an area outside to play the game. Select three players. Designate one player to hold the egg carton. Another player, with back toward the trash can, tosses the eggs backward, over his or her head, into the trash can, and another player quotes the memory verse.

Game Instructions:

Players designated to quote the memory verse open the game by saying the verse.

Each time the scripture is quoted correctly, the player holding the egg carton gives an egg to the player designated to toss.

The player designated to toss, with back toward the trash can, and without looking back, tosses the egg backward, over his/her head, into the trash can.

Each time the scripture is quoted correctly, another egg can be tossed.

The person/team with the most eggs in the trash can, or in closest proximity to the trash can, wins.

Optional: Positions can rotate to give each player an opportunity to say the memory verse.

Game Goal:

Symbolize getting rid of the old, stinky past by tossing the eggs behind you.

Final Word:

Every week, we take out the trash. There's a lot of stuff in the trash that's from the past. The food that smelled fine last week doesn't smell so great, now! In the same way, we can't enjoy the awesome future God has for us if the smelly past is still hanging around, can we? Let's forget the old, no-good stuff, and reach for God's best. It's out in front of us!

Variation: Alternative Eggs

Here are a few alternatives to real eggs:

Plastic Easter eggs are easy to clean up and can allow kids to write down and insert in the eggs, things they'd like to forget and toss away.

Wads of newspaper or recycling paper with things to forget written on them, can also be a powerful demonstration of "throwing out" the past.

Notes: _____
_____
_____
_____
_____
_____
_____
_____
_____
_____
_____
_____
_____
_____
_____
_____
_____
_____
_____
_____

Home Bible Study for Kids • Week 8: ALL OF MY PAST

ACTIVITY PAGE — LIVING WATER PUZZLE

Memory Verse: But I focus on this one thing: Forgetting the past and looking forward to what lies ahead.
—Philippians 3:13

This week's Bible Lesson took place at the town well. Citizens visited the well every day to draw water for cooking, drinking and washing. On the day the Samaritan woman went to the well, she found a new kind of water—living water from Jesus. It was just one more time Jesus untangled someone's life and introduced him or her to The Sweet Life.

In this puzzle, see if you can untangle the ropes and discover which well holds the bucket filled with water.

Series: Sweet Life

WEEK 9: ALL OF MY PRESENT

- **DAY 1: BIBLE LESSON—THE PARABLE OF THE 10 BRIDESMAIDS** ▶ PG 128

- **DAY 2: READ-ALOUD—B-RAD'S EXCELLENT ADVENTURE, PART 5: "FLYING COCONUTS"** ▶ PG 130

- **DAY 3: GIVING LESSON—TIME TO GET STARTED** ▶ PG 133

- **DAY 4: OBJECT LESSON—MAKE TIME FOR GOD** ▶ PG 134

- **DAY 5: GAME TIME—BREAKFAST RUSH** ▶ PG 135

- **BONUS: ACTIVITY PAGE—PARABLE OF THE BRIDESMAIDS WORD SEARCH** ▶ PG 137

Memory Verse: The "right time" is now. Today is the day of salvation. —2 Corinthians 6:2

Home Bible Study for Kids • Week 9: ALL OF MY PRESENT

WEEK 9: SNAPSHOT — ALL OF MY PRESENT

DAY	TYPE OF LESSON	LESSON TITLE	SUPPLIES
Day 1	Bible Lesson	The Parable of the 10 Bridesmaids	None
Day 2	Read-Aloud	B-Rad's Excellent Adventure, Part 5: "Flying Coconuts"	None
Day 3	Giving Lesson	Time to Get Started	Several fliers (pamphlets) created to advertise services that can be provided by your kids (ex: dogwalking, lawnmowing, babysitting, housecleaning, etc.)
Day 4	Object Lesson	Make Time for God	1 Clear plastic jar, 1 Clear pitcher (filled with dried beans), 3 Small colorful balls that will fit easily into the clear plastic jar
Day 5	Game Time	Breakfast Rush	3 Large clear glasses filled with chocolate milk, 3 Donuts (placed on napkins), 3 Bananas, 1 Table, 3 Chairs, Small donuts or donut holes for everyone (optional), Upbeat music
Bonus	Activity Page	Parable of the Bridesmaids Word Search	1 Copy for each child

Lesson Introduction:

This can be a somewhat serious message, but you don't need to make it scary. Emphasize the reward for readiness—staying prepared to serve God. It's obvious in this week's lesson, that God wants to reward us, big-time! The purpose of the story is not to create fear or worried questions about preparedness. Instead, it can be used as a reminder of how God has a reunion planned with His family. Confessing Him as Lord of your life, believing He died on the cross for the forgiveness of our sins, and that He rose again to reunite us with God the Father, is the only "ticket" we need!

Will you ask God each day what He would like you to do?

Would you tell the Lord that you will reach out to someone who needs kindness today?

Can we promise Jesus He can count on us to be a light today?

Invite your kids to make this commitment with you. Then, you *will* be prepared!

Commander Dana
—Commander Dana

Series: Sweet Life

Home Bible Study for Kids • Week 9: ALL OF MY PRESENT

Lesson Outline:

There's no better time than right now to serve God and live wholeheartedly for Him. Encourage your kids to live with passion for God and not dwell on the past or worry about the future. Instead, instruct them to focus on today—what God has called them to do, right now. Their heavenly Father has important work for them to do in their homes, schools, neighborhoods and churches. He needs them to be serious about their relationship with Him and The Sweet Life He has given them. They can be mighty ministers for Him, no matter what age they are.

I. GOD IS A "RIGHT-NOW" GOD

    a. God knows our past and our future. 2 Timothy 1:9

    b. The Word of God says our future is secure.

    c. Today is always the best time to serve God. 2 Corinthians 6:2

II. DON'T WAIT TOO LONG

    a. Ten girls were invited to attend a wedding. Matthew 25:1-12

    b. Five did not stay ready and were left out.

    c. God's Word says that being ready is being wise.

III. BE READY, RIGHT NOW, TO SERVE GOD

    a. Jesus said we should stay ready for His return. Matthew 25:13

    b. God rewards children who serve Him, right now!

    c. Will you stay ready to live for God every day?

Notes:_____
_____
_____
_____
_____
_____
_____

Series: Sweet Life

Home Bible Study for Kids • Week 9: ALL OF MY PRESENT

DAY 1: BIBLE LESSON — THE PARABLE OF THE 10 BRIDESMAIDS

Memory Verse: The "right time" is now. Today is the day of salvation. —2 Corinthians 6:2

Traditionally some believers have used this passage to invoke a sense of, "I've got to work hard to be ready." Being prepared does not mean performing a list of good works in order to get to heaven. Be challenged today as you read this story, and remind your children that being ready is similar to packing your bag for a sleepover at Grandma's house. You prepare for the event before Grandma arrives, so she doesn't have to wait for you, and because you anticipate her coming with delight, there is no fear!

If your kids are older, you can relate the situation to actually being in a wedding. It would be very strange to be part of a wedding and not have a shower and clean clothes and be prepared for the party. It's the same in this situation with Jesus. Being ready is a simple process. God isn't trying to catch us unprepared or doing the wrong thing. He's giving us the plan, telling us how it works and how to prepare ourselves. He's also warning us that lots of people want to celebrate and go to the party, but in order to do that, some preparation is necessary.

Watch your kids' faith grow as they walk out their trust in Jesus and His provision for a "Sweet Life" filled with His goodness, based on Him, not our good works!

Read Matthew 25:1-13:

Then the Kingdom of Heaven will be like ten bridesmaids who took their lamps and went to meet the bridegroom.

Five of them were foolish, and five were wise.

The five who were foolish didn't take enough olive oil for their lamps, but the other five were wise enough to take along extra oil. When the bridegroom was delayed, they all became drowsy and fell asleep. At midnight they were roused by the shout, "Look, the bridegroom is coming! Come out and meet him!"

All the bridesmaids got up and prepared their lamps. Then the five foolish ones asked the others, "Please give us some of your oil because our lamps are going out."

But the others replied, "We don't have enough for all of us. Go to a shop and buy some for yourselves."

But while they were gone to buy oil, the bridegroom came. Then those who were ready went in with him to the marriage feast, and the door was locked. Later, when the other five bridesmaids returned, they stood outside, calling, "Lord! Lord! Open the door for us!"

But he called back, "Believe me, I don't know you!"

So you, too, must keep watch! For you do not know the day or hour of my return.

Discussion Questions:

1. How many bridesmaids were there?
   There were 10—five wise and five foolish.

Series: Sweet Life

2. **Why were some called wise and some called foolish?**
   The wise bridesmaids had enough oil for their lamps, and the foolish ones did not.

3. **What happened when the bridegroom came in the middle of the night?**
   The foolish bridesmaids asked for oil from the wise bridesmaids.

4. **Did the wise bridesmaids give some of their oil to the foolish ones? Why or why not?**
   No, the wise bridesmaids did not give their oil to the foolish ones, because then they wouldn't have had enough for themselves. Instead, they told them to go buy some oil for themselves.

5. **What can I learn from this story?**
   Answers will vary, but we must all understand that no one else is responsible for our faith in Jesus, except ourselves. Our preparation is to love and believe in Jesus and accept Him as our Lord and Savior. That is the preparation for the wedding feast!

6. **What did Jesus mean by saying, "...for you do not know the day or the hour"?**
   Jesus will return for His people, but no one knows the moment of His coming. We do know that faith in Him prepares us for that day. In the meantime we are to live "ready" by following Him, obeying the Holy Spirit and honoring the Word of God.

Notes:

Home Bible Study for Kids • Week 9: ALL OF MY PRESENT

DAY 2: READ-ALOUD — B-RAD'S EXCELLENT ADVENTURE, PART 5: "FLYING COCONUTS"

 **Suggested Time:** 15 minutes

 **Memory Verse:** The "right time" is now. Today is the day of salvation. —2 Corinthians 6:2

 **Background:** This week concludes the five-week read-aloud series, "All of Me," about a writer's discussions of his developing story with his younger friend Tyson, a surfer with a dry sense of humor, who's slightly sarcastic, but all in fun. At the end of this five-week series, the audience will discover that the "Writer" is really B-Rad himself. This story is loosely based on the life of the Apostle Paul. This story includes fun surfing lingo. The unusual terms are defined in parentheses.

Story:

"What's crackillating, dude?" Tyson called out, as he approached his friend who was writing in the margins of his notebook.

The writer squinted up at his friend from under an open umbrella. "Ha! I can trust you for an unusual distraction. Crackillating? That's not exactly surfer lingo, dude!" he chuckled.

"Aww, I thought I'd see if you'd go agro (aggressive) on me when you're beat and bored with your story," Tyson stated as he tossed his board in the sand. He stretched out his lean, tanned arms and crossed them under his head, cushioning himself on the smooth, hard board.

"You're a welcome distraction right now, man. Want an iced tea?" The writer slid his small cooler over to his friend. "'Cuz I'm sure you're going to want to hear the next part in my story, right?"

"Why else would I be hanging here instead of ridin' a boglius (cool, awesome) wave?" Tyson responded. "So, what's up with B-Rad? Are the BAD surfers gonna take him down?"

The writer gazed out at the sea before continuing. "Well, that's it. B-Rad knew God would be with him since He'd told him to reach out to the BAD surfers. No one was hanging on their beach, so he went home. The End."

Tyson jumped to his feet. "LAME-O! That is NOT the ending, dude."

The writer laughed again. "Of course not. GOTCHA! Well, BAD surfers were ready for B-Rad and were hoping they'd get a chance to pound on him a little."

"Yikes! Seriously uncool."

"Well, B-Rad isn't exactly the most well-liked guy by these surfers. Anyways, as they rounded the path that led up to the BAD surfer shack, coconuts started flying from every direction. BAD surfers were in full-force attack mode, trying to nail B-Rad with a painful wallop to his head."

"No way!" Tyson interjected. "They'd better take off while they can."

The writer smiled and said, "You'd think the BAD surfers would do just that, but instead, they didn't bolt and run. The next thing that happened was totally God. I mean it was doke (unbelievable, awesome) all the way. "

Series: Sweet Life

Home Bible Study for Kids • Week 9: ALL OF MY PRESENT

"YESSSSSSS?????" Tyson spoke impatiently. "Focus on the facts, man!"

"Truly, it was a miracle," the writer began. "The BAD surfers had called in reinforcements and were hurling coconuts over broken boards and old, abandoned wood when suddenly Chuck, one of their top dogs, was hit in the head with a coconut by one of his friends. He quit breathing, turning blue in a flash. Coconuts fell to the ground as BAD surfers rushed to help. Right then and there, B-Rad rushed over to Chuck, put his hands on him and started praying! He didn't even take the time to start CPR, he just asked God to touch Chuck.

"Chuck sat up, took a deep breath, and rubbed the bruise developing on the side of his head. An amazing miracle had taken place right before their eyes!"

Tyson spoke. "So did B-Rad start preaching the good news, or what?"

"He told them that now was the right time to let Jesus into their lives and they shouldn't wait another day. He told them yesterday is over and today is all you've got."

"Awesome, dude!" Tyson whistled and then stopped short. "Wait, this story isn't real, is it? I mean, you couldn't have come up with all that on your own. You're not that creative."

"Thanks, a lot."

Tyson laughed. "No, man, seriously, how did you know so much about this B-Rad guy?"

The writer smiled. "That's easy. I'm him."

"Whoa!"

"God does whatever He needs to in order to reach people, man! Chuck's experience was a pretty good visual aid, ya know?" Then the writer stuck his pencil back into his notebook and stood up. "Let's go ride a barrel before someone dubs us froobs (someone who can't ride a wave)."

"What?" Tyson laughed, "Now, you're a surfer too? You gotta be kidding me. That'll be grand if you actually know what you're doing. I'm looking for a kamikaze wave."

The writer yelled over his shoulder as he raced out into the foaming surf, "Not if I beat you to it!"

THE END

Discussion Questions:

Use these questions as conversation starters. Enjoy this time of heart-to-heart conversation with your children.

1. Do you think B-Rad had any idea when he first received Jesus what God had in store for him or to whom he would minister first?
2. How did God prepare him for his assignment?
3. What would have happened if B-Rad had ignored God's leading to become a surfer?
4. Do you think his opinion about surfers changed? How?
5. What have you learned from this series so far?

Home Bible Study for Kids • Week 9: ALL OF MY PRESENT

Notes:

Series: Sweet Life

Home Bible Study for Kids • Week 9: ALL OF MY PRESENT

DAY 3: GIVING LESSON — TIME TO GET STARTED

Suggested Time: 10 minutes

Offering Scripture: You lazy fool, look at an ant. Watch it closely; let it teach you a thing or two. Nobody has to tell it what to do. All summer it stores up food; at harvest it stockpiles provisions. So how long are you going to laze around doing nothing? —Proverbs 6:6-8, MSG

Supplies: ☐ Several fliers (pamphlets) created to advertise services that can be provided by your kids (ex: dogwalking, lawnmowing, babysitting, housecleaning, etc.)

Lesson Instructions:

Today, I want to pass along to you some instructions from our Manual (the Bible). In Proverbs 6:6-8, MSG, it says, "You lazy fool, look at an ant. Watch it closely; let it teach you a thing or two. Nobody has to tell it what to do. All summer it stores up food; at harvest it stockpiles provisions. So how long are you going to laze around doing nothing?"

Wow, those are pretty strong words, aren't they?

Maybe you're thinking, *That's talking to grown-ups, they're the ones who need to work.* Not necessarily. God wants His kids to know how to work hard and get things done too! I don't mean for you to go out and get a job at a pizza place or at the bank down the street. However, there are "jobs" that boys and girls your age can do. Let's talk about a few ideas.

Let's make some fliers that can help you be more like the ant. Maybe you've seen some like these hanging on bulletin boards at the grocery store or the ice cream shop. The fliers work great to advertise kid-friendly jobs you can do to earn money and be a help to family and friends.

Let's see if there is something *you* can do!

Display sample fliers, and briefly describe the job or service advertised on each one.

You can post these at home or maybe give them to relatives and neighbors.

Of course, I'll help on your job hunt. At first, the thought of doing work may not sound like a lot of fun, but after you get started, you'll find out that those tiny ants know a little secret. It feels great to work hard and get things done. It's especially cool to have some money in your pocket that you've earned yourself. And, guess what? When you bring a tithe and offering from the money you've worked hard for, both you and God know it's just a little different. That's because it's coming from your time spent acting like the wise ant!

Notes: _____
_____
_____
_____

Home Bible Study for Kids • Week 9: ALL OF MY PRESENT

DAY 4: OBJECT LESSON — MAKE TIME FOR GOD

Suggested Time: 10 minutes

Memory Verse: The "right time" is now. Today is the day of salvation. —2 Corinthians 6:2

Supplies: ☐ 1 Clear, plastic jar, ☐ 1 Clear pitcher (filled with dried beans), ☐ 3 Small, colorful balls that will fit easily into the clear, plastic jar

Prior to Lesson:

Try this on your own before doing it for the kids.

First, place the three, small, colorful balls into the jar.

Next, fill the jar to the top with the dried pinto beans (pouring the beans over the balls).

Filling the jar with beans after the balls have been placed inside, will assure the right amount of beans required for the demonstration.

The beans fill up the space around the balls. When the beans are added first, the balls won't fit into the jar.

Lesson Instructions:

I've been noticing how busy everyone is lately.

Have you noticed that too?

It seems like there are so many people to see, places to go and things to do! Sometimes a day can be so busy that some of the most important things get left out. *(Hold up the jar, the pitcher of beans and the three balls.)*

These beans represent all the things you have to do each day. *(Pour some of the beans into the jar.)*

You wake up in the morning and think, *When I get all my other stuff done, I'll spend time with God.* You eat breakfast, you go to school, go to basketball practice and then come home. *(Pour more beans into the jar.)* Then, you do homework or chores, eat dinner and play some games with your family. *(Pour the remaining beans into the jar.)*

Before you know it, it's bedtime. That's when you realize you're out of time. It's too late. *(Try to fit the balls into the jar.)* Now you've spent your whole day doing other things, and have no room left in your day for God. *(Empty the beans from the jar back into the pitcher.)*

Now, let's see what happens when you put your time with God first! *(Place the three balls into the empty jar, and slowly pour the beans into the jar as the lesson continues.)* You spend time with God, you eat your breakfast, go to school, practice basketball, come home, do your homework, eat dinner and play some games with your family. *(Display the jar, with the balls and the beans both fitting inside.)*

Look at that! When you put your time with God first, everything else falls into place! Kids, you can make up your mind to always put time with God first place. When you do, everything else fits much better!

Series: Sweet Life

Home Bible Study for Kids • Week 9: ALL OF MY PRESENT

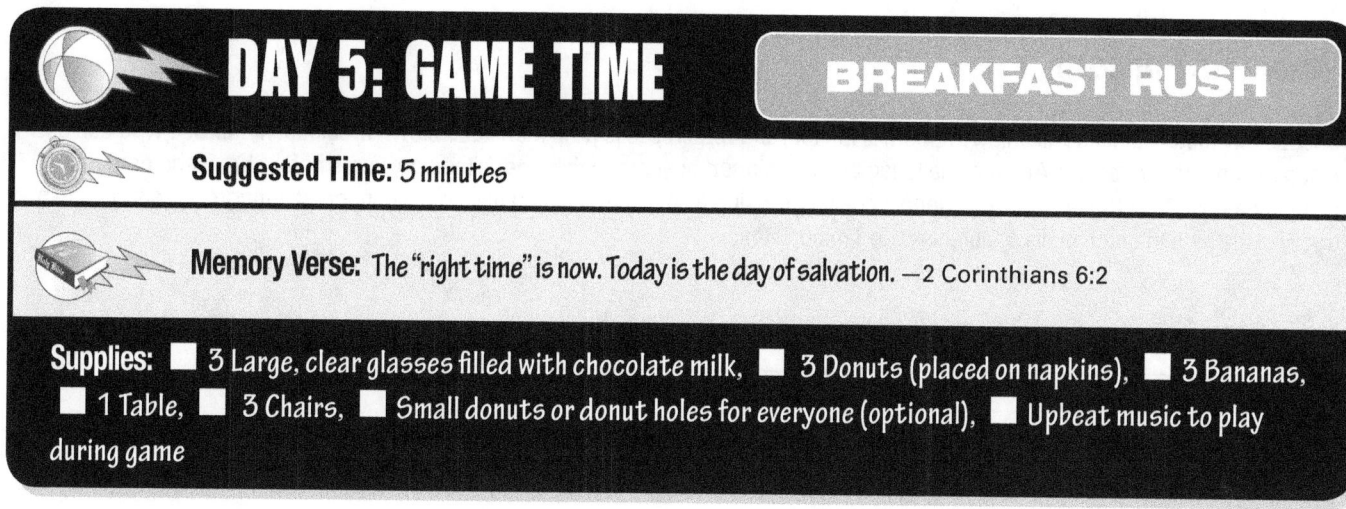

DAY 5: GAME TIME — BREAKFAST RUSH

Suggested Time: 5 minutes

Memory Verse: The "right time" is now. Today is the day of salvation. —2 Corinthians 6:2

Supplies:
- [ ] 3 Large, clear glasses filled with chocolate milk
- [ ] 3 Donuts (placed on napkins)
- [ ] 3 Bananas
- [ ] 1 Table
- [ ] 3 Chairs
- [ ] Small donuts or donut holes for everyone (optional)
- [ ] Upbeat music to play during game

Prior to Game:

Set the "breakfast table" with the breakfast items divided evenly and placed on both sides of table.

Game Instructions:

How many of you like to eat breakfast? Of course, the usual time for breakfast is in the morning after we wake up, but I'm kind of hungry, now.

So, who else is hungry right now? Great! Because we're going to have a breakfast challenge!

Choose 3 players.

Have players decide the order in which they will eat their breakfast items.

The first "diner" will sit on the chair and eat his/her breakfast.

When finished, the first diner gets up and allows the next player to sit and eat his/her breakfast, and so on, until all diners have had a turn.

Game Goal:

The person who eats breakfast fastest, wins.

Final Word:

Did I save you from hunger today?

Did you know that God's Word says that today is the right time for salvation?

It's true! It's written in 2 Corinthians 6:2. The best thing about God is He doesn't wait. He's a right-now God. So, if you're hungry, you don't have to wait until morning, now you can eat breakfast morning, noon or night!

Series: Sweet Life

Variation: Popcorn

Choose any food your kids will enjoy. Popcorn is fun too, and requires less prep than a full-blown breakfast meal! See who can eat a cup of popcorn the fastest. Add the challenge that the winner must recite the week's memory verse before he or she can truly be the champion! For those who really need a challenge, using a timer, see how many kernels of popped popcorn a teammate can throw in the air and catch in his or her mouth in 1 minute. Enjoy!

Notes: _____

_____

_____

_____

_____

_____

_____

_____

_____

_____

_____

_____

_____

_____

_____

_____

_____

_____

_____

_____

_____

Home Bible Study for Kids • Week 9: ALL OF MY PRESENT

ACTIVITY PAGE

PARABLE OF THE BRIDESMAIDS WORD SEARCH

Memory Verse: The "right time" is now. Today is the day of salvation. —2 Corinthians 6:2

This week, you've learned how important it is to live life with a spiritual readiness. It's not hard to do, it only requires that you love and serve Jesus as your Lord and Savior. This week's Bible Lesson told you the parable Jesus used to instruct people in this message. Now, it's your turn to pay close attention and find 12 words from that story.

PARABLE OF THE BRIDESMAIDS WORD SEARCH

```
Q M F D X U R P O S S M A R R I A G E Q P E
G N G S L E X N G D L W O N G A L S G T F M
P L A M P I C B I Z K E O B H Z A H H I K O
E V J X M H D A J X M L I O J M O G L X M O
E C K D S T M A L T N T T C D D I E K D N R
L X L E J S V H L S J Y Y E L N J P L E J G
S Z P F E R E H P A H S F T D V I F P V I E
I A O D S O L I V E O I A I E T Y O O F O D
T S I I I O H C I F R O M A I R U L I R U I
A R U H W P N D U B H P P E U B H D U B H R
B F Y T D R O W S Y E P A F H S I L O O F B
```

- BRIDEGROOM
- BRIDESMAIDS
- DROWSY
- FEAST
- FOOLISH
- LAMP
- MARRIAGE
- MIDNIGHT
- OIL
- OLIVE
- SLEEP
- WISE

Series: Sweet Life

Home Bible Study for Kids • Week 9: ALL OF MY PRESENT

ANSWER KEY

PARABLE OF THE BRIDESMAIDS WORD SEARCH

```
Q M F D X U R P O S S M A R R I A G E Q P E
G N G S L E X N G D L W O N G A L S G T F M
P L A M P I C B I Z K E O B H Z A H H I K O
E V J X M H D A J X M L I O J M O G L X M O
E C K D S T M A L T N T T C D D I E K D N R
L X L E J S V H L S J Y Y E L N J P L E J G
S Z P F E R E H P A H S F T D V I F P V I E
I A O D S O L I V E O I A I E T Y O O F O D
T S I I I O H C I F R O M A I R U L I R U I
A R U H W P N D U B H P P E U B H D U B H R
B F Y T D R O W S Y E P A F H S I L O O F B
```

BRIDEGROOM	FOOLISH	OIL
BRIDESMAIDS	LAMP	OLIVE
DROWSY	MARRIAGE	SLEEP
FEAST	MIDNIGHT	WISE

Notes: _____
_____
_____
_____
_____
_____
_____
_____
_____

WEEK 10: ALL OF MY FUTURE

 DAY 1: BIBLE LESSON—THE GOOD SAMARITAN ▶ PG 142

 DAY 2: REAL DEAL—FLORENCE NIGHTINGALE ▶ PG 144

 DAY 3: GIVING LESSON—LET IT RISE ▶ PG 147

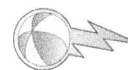 DAY 4: FOOD FUN—FOLLOW THE RECIPE ▶ PG 148

 DAY 5: GAME TIME—CHEESE RUN ▶ PG 150

 BONUS: ACTIVITY PAGE—MISSING ELEMENTS ▶ PG 151

Memory Verse: Seek his will in all you do, and he will show you which path to take. —Proverbs 3:6

Home Bible Study for Kids • Week 10: ALL OF MY FUTURE

WEEK 10: SNAPSHOT — ALL OF MY FUTURE

DAY	TYPE OF LESSON	LESSON TITLE	SUPPLIES
Day 1	Bible Lesson	The Good Samaritan	None
Day 2	Real Deal	Florence Nightingale	**Optional costume/prop:** Old-fashioned dress (can be found at a thrift store), Hair in a neat low bun, Hand-held lamp or candle
Day 3	Giving Lesson	Let It Rise	1 Small helium-filled balloon (can be heart-shaped), 1 Air-filled balloon for each child, 1 Black permanent marker, 1 Large trash bag
Day 4	Food Fun	Follow the Recipe	2-4 Parfait glasses or dessert dishes, 1 Medium-sized mixing bowl, 1 Wire whisk, A large spoon, 1 Rolling pin, 1 Small resealable plastic storage bag, Plastic spoons, 1 Apron each for the chef and sous-chefs, 1 Small box of vanilla instant pudding, 2 Cups of cold milk, 1 Small package of cream-filled sandwich cookies, 1 Can of pressurized whipped cream
Day 5	Game Time	Cheese Run	1 Table, 2 Plates, 1 Bowl, Crackers, 2 Cans of a "squirt-type" cheese, Upbeat music
Bonus	Activity Page	Missing Elements	1 Copy for each child

Lesson Introduction:

Traveling to many churches the last few years, has given me the opportunity to meet a large number of great leaders. I've noticed that sometimes people become so busy working to serve God that His priorities are lost in the process. I once heard a well-meaning pastor say, "I don't have time to be nice." Wow.

Let me challenge you to stop and think for a moment about that comment! God has no priority greater than His family, and you and I are in contact with them every day. Jesus said the greatest commandment after loving God was to love our neighbor. And who is our neighbor? According to Luke 10, it's the person we meet who has a need. Busy priests and Levites didn't have time. Will you be too busy to keep the greatest commandment?

Determine right now to be the "neighbor" who touches and blesses God's family. Great is your reward!

Commander Dana
—Commander Dana

Series: Sweet Life

Lesson Outline:

God has a plan for your children. He wants to use them in mighty ways for the kingdom of God. Sometimes, people think they will serve God "one day" in the future. They want to enjoy the ways of the world today and get serious about following God later in life. But the future, like everything else, belongs to God. Your children's heavenly Father has a plan for them, and He needs your children to do all He's called them to do in the present *and* the future.

I. GOD HAS A GREAT FUTURE FOR HIS KIDS

    a. God is the best Planner ever.

    b. God knew all about you before He made the world! 2 Timothy 1:9

    c. God has been thinking about you for a long, long time.

II. THERE IS A RACE FOR US TO RUN Hebrews 12:1

    a. Our race lasts as long as we live on the earth.

    b. Jesus is the judge of the race we run. 2 Timothy 4:7-8

    c. There is a great reward for finishing this race. Philippians 3:14

III. FINISH THE RACE, WIN YOUR FUTURE

    a. Jesus told the two main secrets of winning.

    b. Secret No. 1: Love God! Matthew 22:36-38

    c. Secret No. 2: Love people! Matthew 22:39

Notes: _____

_____

_____

_____

_____

_____

_____

_____

Home Bible Study for Kids • Week 10: ALL OF MY FUTURE

DAY 1: BIBLE LESSON — THE GOOD SAMARITAN

Memory Verse: *Seek his will in all you do, and he will show you which path to take.* —Proverbs 3:6

So often, people get involved in different ministries and then get caught up trying to figure out what tasks are most important to God. But the things that matter most to God are clearly spelled out in Matthew 22. God wants us to love Him, and then love those around us. If we do those two things, all that is important to Jesus will be accomplished, and the needs of people (physical, spiritual and emotional) will be met.

Read Luke 10:25-37:

One day an expert in religious law stood up to test Jesus by asking him this question: "Teacher, what should I do to inherit eternal life?"

Jesus replied, "What does the law of Moses say? How do you read it?"

The man answered, "'You must love the Lord your God with all your heart, all your soul, all your strength, and all your mind.' And, 'Love your neighbor as yourself.'"

"Right!" Jesus told him. "Do this and you will live!"

The man wanted to justify his actions, so he asked Jesus, "And who is my neighbor?"

Parable of the Good Samaritan

Jesus replied with a story: "A Jewish man was traveling from Jerusalem down to Jericho, and he was attacked by bandits. They stripped him of his clothes, beat him up, and left him half dead beside the road.

"By chance a priest came along. But when he saw the man lying there, he crossed to the other side of the road and passed him by. A Temple assistant walked over and looked at him lying there, but he also passed by on the other side.

"Then a despised Samaritan came along, and when he saw the man, he felt compassion for him. Going over to him, the Samaritan soothed his wounds with olive oil and wine and bandaged them. Then he put the man on his own donkey and took him to an inn, where he took care of him. The next day he handed the innkeeper two silver coins, telling him, 'Take care of this man. If his bill runs higher than this, I'll pay you the next time I'm here.'

"Now which of these three would you say was a neighbor to the man who was attacked by bandits?" Jesus asked.

The man replied, "The one who showed him mercy."

Then Jesus said, "Yes, now go and do the same."

Discussion Questions:

1. **What did Jesus say were the two most important commandments?**
   He said first to love God with your heart, soul, strength and mind. Then, He said to love your neighbor as yourself.

2. **What happened in the story Jesus told?**
   Allow children to retell the story in their own words. Be sure they include the two people who passed by the injured man, noting the one who stopped.

3. **What is the significance of a Samaritan helping a Jew?**
   Historically, these two people groups were very prejudiced against each other and did not socialize or interact. In fact, they tried to avoid one another.

4. **What did the Samaritan do?**
   He stopped to help. He bandaged the injured man's wounds and had compassion on him. Then, he took him to a place to recover and paid for the man's care until he was well.

5. **What message was Jesus saying at the end of this story?**
   He told us to go and be like the Samaritan!

6. **Can you think of a time when you were like the Good Samaritan? Or when you wanted to do something for someone because you felt compassion for them? How did that feel?**
   Accept reasonable answers, and enjoy this time of discussion.

7. **Is there something in your heart that you would like to do for someone else, now?**
   Take time to share and see if your family can take action.

8. **Was Jesus saying we don't need the commandments of Moses?**
   No, He was saying that if we love God and our neighbor, we will inadvertently keep all the Old Testament commandments because they are summed up in these two New Testament commands.

Variation: Service

Consider choosing a family service project like:

- Reaching out to neighbors, especially the elderly or single-parent families, by offering to cut their lawns, weed their flower gardens, help with home maintenance or take their dogs for a walk.
- Collecting cans of food for your church's or city's food pantry.
- Entering a walk-a-thon to raise money for a worthy cause.
- Asking your church's pastoral staff for ways to meet needs in your congregation.

Notes: _____
_____
_____
_____
_____
_____
_____
_____
_____
_____

Home Bible Study for Kids • Week 10: ALL OF MY FUTURE

DAY 2: REAL DEAL — FLORENCE NIGHTINGALE

 **Memory Verse:** Seek his will in all you do, and he will show you which path to take. —Proverbs 3:6

 **Concept:** Highlighting an interesting historical place, figure or event that illustrates the theme of the day. The theme of the day is allowing God to plan your future.

 **Media:** If you have technical capability, show a DVD about Florence Nightingale (sometimes available at your local library; also free videos available to download online). If you do not have this capability, you may print out pictures from the Internet to show what Florence looked like.

Optional Costume/Prop: ☐ Old-fashioned dress (can be found at a thrift store), ☐ Hair in a neat, low bun, ☐ Hand-held lamp or candle

Intro:

Today we're talking about the future—your future. God is the best Planner, and He has a great plan for every one of His kids. There is one lady who knew this for a fact. As a 17-year-old, she realized God was calling her to serve Him by loving people. How did she accomplish that? She became the first great nurse of the modern world and the founder of modern nursing. She was called the "Lady With the Lamp" *(hold up your lamp)*.

Do you know who she was?

Lesson Instructions:
Not Everyone Likes God's Plan:

The amazing young girl I'm talking about is Florence Nightingale. She was born in 1820 to a very wealthy, influential and popular British couple. Both Florence and her sister were taught by expensive private teachers as well as by their father. Florence was a great student, and she loved learning, which eventually helped her accomplish the goals God had set for her. One of her favorite things to do was write, and she was always writing in her diary. In fact, that's where she wrote down God's plan for her life. God asked her if she would do good for Him, without caring what other people thought. However, when Florence shared this with her family, they were not at all excited. In fact, they were very upset and angry. Her mother was the most difficult of all her family. She wanted Florence to do other things with her life, like throw big parties for important people. Why wasn't Florence's family excited about God's plan for her life?

It was simple, really. Back then, being a nurse was one of the worst jobs a person could have. Nurses worked with poor, sick and dirty people. They made very little money. Not exactly the kind of thing a rich, popular girl should do—or so her family thought.

It was a good thing Florence had decided not to care about what others thought. She stepped out boldly to follow God's plan, anyway.

Series: Sweet Life

A Big Need:

During this period of time, there were no training programs for nurses. They simply learned by practice and intuition with no formal education or scientific knowledge. Imagine working in a hospital without any medical training! Hospitals were mostly places for poor people who couldn't afford private medical care. They were dirty, smelly and overcrowded. Most hospitals had very bad sewer systems that wouldn't drain. With no airflow in the building, you can imagine how stinky and unsanitary things were! Hospitals were known as a place for people to come and die, while nurses fed and bathed them. They were not considered places to get well.

This didn't scare Florence. She jumped right in and became a nurse, without receiving any pay. Florence didn't like the conditions of the hospitals, so she began to work hard to clean them and make improvements. That was a big job, but once things were clean, she noticed less people died and more people got better. It was amazing! At that time, no one knew about the effect of germs on the body, but God gave Florence some hidden keys to healing. This improved people's opinions of hospitals.

Florence was promoted and became the head nurse in London.

The Lady With the Lamp:

So, how did Florence receive the nickname, "Lady With the Lamp"?

During the Crimean War, she led a team of nurses to help wounded soldiers. Once again, Florence sprang into action to clean up the disgusting and dangerously dirty hospitals. Almost half the soldiers had died from germs because things were so dirty. Because of Florence's hard work, after the cleaning, most of the soldiers survived!

But cleaning hospitals wasn't Florence's only mission. She knew God had called her to love and care for people. So every night, when all the doctors and other nurses went home to sleep, Florence would light her lamp and visit the soldiers, one by one. She encouraged them, listened to their stories and brought them hope. One newspaper even called her a "ministering angel." That's how she became known as the "Lady With the Lamp." She was so determined to run the race God had planned for her that she chose to work 20 exhausting hours every day for a time. Only four hours of sleep each night!

Making History:

Florence was faithful with the little jobs God gave her when she started out as a volunteer nurse without pay. But the Bible promises that when we're faithful with a little, God will entrust us with more! Eventually, she became known as the greatest nurse in the world, and here's why:

- Training and Building: Florence wrote two training books that were used to teach hospitals. She also became an expert on designing hospitals. She began the Nightingale Training School for Nurses. The nurses who trained at this school were called "Nightingale Nurses," and they were the best in the world. Hospitals everywhere wanted to hire them because of their experience and training. Florence sent her nurses all over the world, like missionaries, and they always had a beautiful bouquet of flowers waiting for them upon their arrival.

- Influencing Kings and Queens: Queen Victoria asked Florence to help establish an army medical school and improve the health of England's army. King Edward VII awarded Florence the "Order of Merit" medal. She was the first woman to ever receive this award for being an outstanding servant.

- Impacting America: Florence personally trained America's first nurse, Linda Richards, who went on to become a pioneer of nursing in America and Japan. Linda Richards also helped the U.S. secretary of war establish army hospitals during the Civil War.

Home Bible Study for Kids • Week 10: ALL OF MY FUTURE

- **Impacting the World:** The man who founded the International Red Cross (which cares for the sick, wounded and those hit by disasters) said he did so because he was so inspired by Florence's life!

Outro:

If Florence Nightingale had listened to the people around her, she would have spent her life throwing big parties and pursuing social accolades. Instead, she listened to God and followed the awesome plan He had for her. Florence knew a great secret: Nothing is more fun than loving God and loving people. That's why Florence Nightingale is today's Real Deal.

Notes: _____
_____
_____
_____
_____
_____
_____
_____
_____
_____
_____
_____
_____
_____
_____
_____
_____

Home Bible Study for Kids • Week 10: ALL OF MY FUTURE

DAY 3: GIVING LESSON — LET IT RISE

Suggested Time: 10 minutes

Offering Scripture: Sitting across from the offering box, he was observing how the crowd tossed money in for the collection. Many of the rich were making large contributions. One poor widow came up and put in two small coins—a measly two cents. Jesus called his disciples over and said, "The truth is that this poor widow gave more to the collection than all the others put together. All the others gave what they'll never miss; she gave extravagantly what she couldn't afford— she gave her all." — Mark 12:41-44 MSG

Supplies: ☐ 1 Small helium-filled balloon (can be heart-shaped), ☐ 1 Air-filled balloon for each child, ☐ 1 Black permanent marker ☐ 1 Large trash bag

Prior to Lesson:

Using the black permanent marker, write the word "offering" on each balloon.

Lesson Instructions:

(Enter the room with the air-filled balloons and one helium-filled balloon inside the trash bag. Adjust the number of balloons so each child receives one balloon.)

Does anyone want to guess what's in my bag?

Well, before we see what it is, I want to tell you about a woman who lived long ago and gave all she had.

(Read the story of the "widow's mite" in Mark 12:41-44, MSG. See offering scripture.)

Who would like to help me hold what's in my bag?

I'll let each of you help me with my bag. (Be sure to have one balloon for each child.)

(Let kids peek into the bag. Carefully pull the balloons out of the bag, one by one. Place the balloons in the kids' hands, so that the balloons are tightly held with the knot inside their fists, while the air-filled part of the balloon is appearing to sit on top of each child's fist.)

This reminds me of the story we just read.

A crowd was coming by to drop their offerings one by one into the container. Lots of rich people were throwing in large sums of money so everyone could see, but it wasn't really "costing" them anything because they had so much. They could throw in any amount they wanted. It wasn't hard for the rich to let go of extra money, so they gave without thought.

When the widow threw in the smallest amount of anyone in the crowd, it caught Jesus' attention, so He pulled His disciples aside and taught them a great lesson! The most important thing about your offering is not how much money it is but how much of your heart goes with it.

Because she gave with all her heart, her offering reached the heart of Jesus. So, when we count to three, you will release your balloons. (The air-filled balloons will fall to the floor, while the smallest of them, the helium balloon, will float to the ceiling.)

Jesus wants your offering to be just like the "widow's mite," an offering from your heart that rises to the Father.

Series: Sweet Life

Home Bible Study for Kids • Week 10: ALL OF MY FUTURE

DAY 4: FOOD FUN — FOLLOW THE RECIPE

Suggested Time: 10 minutes

Key Scripture: For God saved us and called us to live a holy life. He did this, not because we deserved it, but because that was his plan from before the beginning of time.... —2 Timothy 1:9

Supplies: ☐ 2-4 Parfait glasses or dessert dishes, ☐ 1 Medium-sized mixing bowl, ☐ 1 Wire whisk, ☐ A large spoon, ☐ 1 Rolling pin, ☐ 1 Small resealable plastic storage bag, ☐ Plastic spoons, ☐ 1 Apron each for the chef and sous-chefs

Prior to Lesson:

Allow your children, or your sous-chefs, to help with this lesson. Let one child read the recipe, step by step, and allow the others to assist with the preparations of the pudding parfaits. It's fun to have aprons for the sous-chefs as well as the chef.

Lesson Instructions:

Thank you for being such great helpers. In professional kitchens, such helpers are called "sous-chefs." You have a very important job today. One of you will read the recipe, while the rest of us prepare some delicious pudding parfaits.

(Have one child read the recipe aloud. Prepare the recipe and continue with the lesson after the parfaits are completed.)

(Acknowledging the child who read the recipe) I'm especially thankful to *(child's name)* helping with the most important part of preparing any dish—the reading of the recipe. We can have all our supplies and every ingredient needed to make a yummy treat, but if the plan or recipe isn't followed, we could end up with a big mess.

Did you know there is someone who has written a great recipe for your life?

That may sound like a funny way to put it, but the Bible tells us that God is a great Planner and He knew all about your life before He even made the world.

Now, since God took the time to write out a recipe for an awesome life for you, wouldn't it be a good idea to follow it?

This way, your life will be nice and sweet, just like this amazing dessert! *(Allow kids to enjoy the treat!)*

Series: Sweet Life

Home Bible Study for Kids • Week 10: ALL OF MY FUTURE

Recipe for Pudding Parfaits:

- ☐ 1 Small box of vanilla instant pudding,
- ☐ 2 Cups of cold milk,
- ☐ 1 Small package of cream-filled sandwich cookies,
- ☐ 1 Can of pressurized whipped cream

1. Beat the instant pudding mix into the 2 cups of cold milk in the mixing bowl with the wire whisk, for 2 minutes.
2. Spoon the mixture into individual serving dishes and allow to set for 5 minutes.
3. Break up the cookies by placing them in the resealable plastic storage bag and use the rolling pin to gently crumble the cookies to the desired consistency—not too small.
4. Now the fun part! To finish up, top the pudding with whipped cream and a generous sprinkling of cookie crumbs.

Notes: _____

Series: Sweet Life

Home Bible Study for Kids • Week 10: ALL OF MY FUTURE

DAY 5: GAME TIME — CHEESE RUN

Suggested Time: 10 minutes

Memory Verse: Seek his will in all you do, and he will show you which path to take. —Proverbs 3:6

Supplies: ☐ 1 Table, ☐ 2 Plates, ☐ A bowl, ☐ Crackers, ☐ 2 Cans of a "squirt-type" cheese, ☐ Upbeat music to play during the game

Prior to Game:

Fill the bowl with crackers and place it in the middle of the table.

Place a plate and pressurized, canned cheese on each side of the bowl.

Game Instructions:

Teach your kids the memory verse.

Line up all the players in 2 teams, 1 team on each side of the table.

On "Go," player 1 grabs a cracker, covers it with cheese, then recites the memory verse.

Once the memory verse is stated correctly, player 1 eats the cheese cracker completely.

Player 1 then returns to the back of the line.

The next player in line repeats the process.

The first team to finish, wins.

Game Goal:

Have fun and feed your crew, while hiding God's Word in their hearts!

Final Word:

When we hide God's Word in our hearts, He will show us which path to take.

Variation No. 1:

Use non-dairy whipped topping on graham crackers for a sweet treat.

Variation No. 2:

If your family is too small to do this as team competition, race one-by-one against the clock to see who can say the verse AND eat the cracker fastest. Those waiting for a turn should wait in a nearby room so they can't hear the Bible verse being recited by game competitors.

Series: Sweet Life

Home Bible Study for Kids • Week 10: ALL OF MY FUTURE

ACTIVITY PAGE — MISSING ELEMENTS

Memory Verse: *Seek his will in all you do, and he will show you which path to take.* —Proverbs 3:6

In the parable of the Good Samaritan, Jesus gave us a key to living a successful Christian life—both in the present and future. He said to "love the Lord your God with all your heart, all your soul, all your strength, and all your mind." And, to "love your neighbor as yourself." Sadly, many people miss these important elements, but you can have 20/20 spiritual vision by putting these two commandments into practice.

The two pictures below look identical, but 10 things are missing from the picture on the right. Find those missing items.

Series: Sweet Life

Home Bible Study for Kids • Week 10: ALL OF MY FUTURE

Notes:

Series: Sweet Life

WEEK 11: FAITH

- **DAY 1: BIBLE LESSON—THE FAITH OF THE ROMAN OFFICER** ▶ PG 156
- **DAY 2: READ-ALOUD—FAITHMAN** ▶ PG 158
- **DAY 3: GIVING LESSON—PROVE IT!** ▶ PG 161
- **DAY 4: ACADEMY LAB—THE HOPE MAGNET** ▶ PG 162
- **DAY 5: GAME TIME—WHAT DO YOU SEE?** ▶ PG 163
- **BONUS: ACTIVITY PAGE—WHAT IS IT? COLOR-BY-SHAPE** ▶ PG 164

Memory Verse: Faith is the confidence that what we hope for will actually happen; it gives us assurance about things we cannot see. —Hebrews 11:1

Home Bible Study for Kids • Week 11: FAITH

WEEK 11: SNAPSHOT — FAITH

DAY	TYPE OF LESSON	LESSON TITLE	SUPPLIES
Day 1	Bible Lesson	The Faith of the Roman Officer	None
Day 2	Read-Aloud	Faithman	None
Day 3	Giving Lesson	Prove It!	10 Pieces of candy, 10 Pieces of another kind of candy, Tray to display candy
Day 4	Academy Lab	The Hope Magnet	1 Large strong magnet, A variety of metal objects that can be drawn to the magnet (ex: paper clips, nails, tacks, fingernail clippers, etc.)
Day 5	Game Time	What Do You See?	Table (with 20-30 miscellaneous items arranged on top); A bedsheet; Whiteboard, dry-erase markers and eraser; or chalkboard, chalk and eraser; or newsprint pad and felt-tip marker; 1 Blindfold for each contestant; Upbeat music
Bonus	Activity Page	What Is It? Color-by-Shape	1 Copy for each child

Lesson Introduction:

This lesson is best illustrated with a bow and arrow (even a polystyrene version is great) or a dartboard of any kind. Ask children to be helpers, and explain the working principles of hope, faith and words as follows: "Boys and girls, there are many things I am hoping for. Today, my hope looks like a target. My faith wants to hit that target for me, but it needs help. This arrow (or dart) is like my faith. It can't really get to that target without being sent there. This bow (or dart) acts just like words. It will send the arrow (dart) wherever it's aimed. Godly words will send faith right where it needs to go. Speaking God's Word will send the faith arrow to the hope target, and WOW! You will have just what you hoped for."

In your illustration, if you happen to miss the target with the arrow or dart, it doesn't really matter. That too, is an opportunity to remind kids that our own arrows can miss, but godly faith arrows never do! God is always right on target!

Commander Dana
—Commander Dana

Series: Sweet Life

Lesson Outline:

Faith is so important to a healthy Christian life because, simply put, faith is believing that God will do what He said He will do. It means that regardless of what the world or circumstances say, we have decided we are going to focus on God and trust Him. God wants His people to be people of faith so that when difficulties come, we won't be discouraged or afraid. Instead, we'll stand strong and confident, knowing that our heavenly Father is always true to His Word.

I. FAITH IS AN AMAZING GIFT FROM HEAVEN James 1:17

    a. Faith is a special gift from God. Romans 12:3

    b. Every person gets the same amount.

    c. Nobody gets a head start, nobody gets left out!

II. FAITH CAN MAKE HOPES AND DREAMS COME TRUE

    a. Can you think of some big dreams you can hope for?
    (Have kids close their eyes and think for 30 seconds, without talking, while they think of their big dreams.)

    b. Share the biggest and best hope you have.

    c. Did you know that your faith aims at what you hope for, and brings it to you?

    d. Faith acts like a "hope magnet"!

III. WORDS AND FAITH WORK LIKE A BOW AND ARROW

    a. Faith is like an arrow aiming at your hope target.

    b. Godly words send the "faith arrow" right to the bull's-eye!

    c. When our dreams are God's dreams, He loves to see them come true!

Notes: _____
_____
_____
_____

Home Bible Study for Kids • Week 11: FAITH

DAY 1: BIBLE LESSON — THE FAITH OF THE ROMAN OFFICER

Memory Verse: Faith is the confidence that what we hope for will actually happen; it gives us assurance about things we cannot see. —Hebrews 11:1

The faith of a child is an amazing thing. Many children are able to hear God's Word and accept it as it is, no questions asked. This week, as you study the biblical principle of faith, allow God to open your eyes to the faith that is already alive and powerfully at work within your family!

Read Luke 7:1-10:

When Jesus had finished saying all this to the people, he returned to Capernaum.

At that time the highly valued slave of a Roman officer was sick and near death. When the officer heard about Jesus, he sent some respected Jewish elders to ask him to come and heal his slave. So they earnestly begged Jesus to help the man. "If anyone deserves your help, he does," they said, "for he loves the Jewish people and even built a synagogue for us."

So Jesus went with them. But just before they arrived at the house, the officer sent some friends to say, "Lord, don't trouble yourself by coming to my home, for I am not worthy of such an honor. I am not even worthy to come and meet you. Just say the word from where you are, and my servant will be healed. I know this because I am under the authority of my superior officers, and I have authority over my soldiers. I only need to say, 'Go,' and they go, or 'Come,' and they come. And if I say to my slaves, 'Do this,' they do it."

When Jesus heard this, he was amazed. Turning to the crowd that was following him, he said, "I tell you, I haven't seen faith like this in all Israel!"

And when the officer's friends returned to his house, they found the slave completely healed.

Discussion Questions:

1. **Who was in need?**
   The Roman officer's servant was sick.

2. **What happened?**
   The Roman officer sent people to ask Jesus to heal his servant.

3. **What did the officer do before Jesus arrived at his house?**
   He sent people to tell Jesus that He didn't need to come in person. The officer knew that if Jesus would speak, the servant would be healed.

4. **How did Jesus respond to this?**
   Jesus said this was the greatest faith in all Israel!

5. **What happened to the servant?**
   He was completely healed.

Series: Sweet Life

6. What does this teach us about faith?
   Faith is believing that God will do what He said He will do.

7. Is there anything that you are believing God for and would like to exercise your faith regarding?
   Take a moment to listen to responses and pray, believing that God will answer your prayers.

Notes: _____

Home Bible Study for Kids • Week 11: FAITH

DAY 2: READ-ALOUD — FAITHMAN

 **Suggested Time:** 15 minutes

 **Memory Verse:** Faith is the confidence that what we hope for will actually happen; it gives us assurance about things we cannot see. —Hebrews 11:1

Story:

Aaron sat morosely, with his chin in his hands. "Man, why can't I just have faith?"

From behind him, he heard a buzzing noise as if something strange were approaching from afar. As the sound drew nearer, Aaron heard an unusual voice answer, "Did I just hear someone say they wanted faith?"

Aaron thought he must be imagining things. Then he looked up to see a guy approaching in a superhero suit, complete with red spandex and a huge "FM" printed in gold across the front of his very tight shirt. Stunned, Aaron asked, "Who are you?"

"So glad you asked!" the guy answered as he dramatically landed directly in front of Aaron with a swoosh of his flashy red cape. "I'm Faithmaaaaaaaaaaaaaaannnnnnnn! Able to remove mountains with a word of faith, faithful partner to Hopeman, and an amazing gift to help kids like you. I'mmmmm Faithmaaaaaaaaannn!"

"Errr, you're a bit strange, too. You're repeating yourself, ya know," Aaron replied with a twitch of laughter. He thought this must be what happens when you drink two sodas and a monster size bag of spicy chips before you go to bed. But, wait! That was hours ago.

Faithman grabbed Aaron's hand and jerked him to his feet. "You must admit it's just so fun to say it, though. You should try introducing yourself like that sometime: 'I'mmmmmmmm Aaaaaaaaaaaaaaron!' C'mon! Try it."

Aaron plopped back into his chair, "Yeah, I guess. Whatever."

With genuine concern, Faithman squatted down beside Aaron's chair. "So, tell me, Aaron—why so gloomy? Why so down in the dumps? You look super sad, man!"

Aaron glanced over at this bizarre guy he was talking to and decided there was nothing to lose. He might as well see what advice this unusual character would share with him. He plunged right to the sore spot, "Well, last week I prayed, and my prayer didn't get answered. I guess I just don't have any faith, or God wasn't interested in what I needed."

Faithman jumped to his feet, alarmed. "This IS an issue for Faithman! I knew it! Hold it *right* there, young man! You don't have any faith?"

Faithman spoke quickly into a fat wristwatch covered in colored buttons and a complex display screen. "Code Red! We have an emergency. No-Faith Zone reported. I repeat, I've hit a No-Faith Zone!" Faithman put his fingers up to Aaron's throat as if to take his pulse. "OK, the good news is, you're still alive!"

Aaron, slightly amused by this absolutely strange visitor, responded with a laugh. "Of course I'm still alive. I just said I didn't have any faith."

"Well," Faithman answered, "you'd be surprised how many people without faith aren't alive, but that strays from our primary

Series: Sweet Life

concern. Moving on! Next question: Have you asked Jesus into your heart?"

Aaron nodded, "Yep."

"Whew!" Faithman began speaking into his wristwatch again. "Hopeman, come in. FM calling HM. Call off the 'No-Faith Zone' alert. We have a false alarm." Turning back to Aaron, he said, "Good news, my boy. You DO have faith!"

Skeptically, Aaron responded, "I do? And exactly how would you know? We've known each other for less than five minutes, man!"

Faithman flashed a quick smile of confidence. "I know because the Superkid Manual, God's Word, tells us that God gave faith as a gift to every believer!"

With a grumpy "Hmph," Aaron answered, "then He must have given me a really small amount of faith."

Faithman bounced around, flinging his cape erratically and snapping Aaron's chair with it. "Wrong again, young whipper-snapper! Every person gets the same amount of faith. Nobody gets a head start, and no one gets left out."

Aaron interrupted, "If that's so, then why didn't my prayer work?"

Faithman bounced around and squatted beside Aaron's chair again. "First things first. There are some things you need to know about faith. Faith and patience are a team. By faith AND patience, you receive God's promises. You need to read Hebrews 6:12."

Impatiently, Aaron asked, "You're avoiding my question. Why didn't my prayer work?"

Very calmly, Faithman sat and smoothed his odd cape behind him. "OK, let me see if I can make it easier for you to understand. Let me think…hmmm. You need to be patient, and let faith do its job."

"But," Aaron interjected, "I'm still not so sure I have the same amount of faith as everybody else. My friend Martin has been a Christian since he was 3. I've only been saved a year. He's got to have more faith than me, because we're supposed to grow in our faith, right?"

"Well, growing in faith doesn't mean that you're getting more and more faith because you've been a Christian for a long time." Faithman fiddled with his flashly "FM" on the front of his shirt.

Aaron was unconvinced. "My pastor knows lots more about the Bible than I do. Doesn't he have more faith?"

Faithman stretched his arms, smoothing his tightly fitted shirt. "Negative! False, wrong, oops, nay and uh-uh. Anything else?"

Aaron hesitated. "There is one more thing…I don't have any special talents, like a lot of other people. Are you sure they don't have more faith than me?"

Faithman stood with a swing of his cape. "As sure as the cape on my back, Aaron. Romans 12:3 says that God has given every person the same amount of faith. Now what you do with it, that's up to you!"

Smiling, Aaron looked up at Faithman. "Thanks, Faithman. I feel better already. Now that I know I have faith, I'm not going to give up on my prayer. I'm just going to keep on believing!"

Faithman patted Aaron on the shoulder. "That's the spirit! By the way, can I ask what you prayed for?"

Aaron glanced at him. "Oh why not? Sure, I prayed and asked God to help me to never have to do homework again."

Smiling, Faithman looked at his new friend carefully. "Well, all I can say is—get used to praying. But before I go, let me give you some awesome Faithman advice. Pray what God's Word says, and you'll get the answer you're looking for every time! So long, Aaron. Until next time, I'mmmmmmm Faithmaaaaaaaaannnnnn!"

Faithman flew away with a swish of his rather unusual cape, leaving Aaron to contemplate the truth of what he'd just heard. This was definitely more than sodas and spicy chips!

THE END

Home Bible Study for Kids • Week 11: FAITH

Discussion Questions:

Use these questions as conversation starters. Enjoy this time of heart-to-heart conversation with your children.

1. What did you learn about faith from this story?
2. Why do you think faith and patience go together?
3. What does it mean to pray God's Word?
4. Parents, share a time when you needed faith and patience for your prayer to be answered.
5. Parents, ask your children if there is anything that you can agree with them in prayer about.

Variation: Prayer Journal

If you have yet to start a family prayer journal with your children, consider doing it now. Record your family's prayer requests and the scriptures on which you will stand for each prayer. Then leave a space for the date it is answered and room to record any significant circumstances surrounding that prayer's answer. Over time, your children will have a wonderful record of God's faithfulness.

Notes: _____
_____
_____
_____
_____
_____
_____
_____
_____
_____
_____
_____
_____
_____
_____
_____

Home Bible Study for Kids • Week 11: FAITH

DAY 3: GIVING LESSON

PROVE IT!

Suggested Time: 10 minutes

Offering Scripture: *Bring ye all the tithes into the storehouse...and prove me now....* —Malachi 3:10 KJV

Supplies: ☐ 10 Pieces of candy, ☐ 10 Pieces of another kind of candy, ☐ Tray to display candy

Prior to Lesson:

Place 10 pieces of the first kind of candy on the tray.

Lesson Instructions:

Hey, kids! It's time to play "Let's Make a Deal!" *(Call a kid by name.)* Come on down! You've been chosen.

The question is, "Will *you* make a deal?"

As you can see, I have here 10 candies. *(Show the tray of candy.)*

I'll give you all 10 of these if you will consider making a deal. Ready?

Here's the deal: I'll give you all 10 pieces of candy, and you only have to give one back. I'll give you time to think.

Do you think this is a good deal?

All right, here are the 10 pieces of candy. *(Show the tray of candy again.)*

Ask contestant No. 1: Will you give one piece back? Will you "Make a Deal"?

(After following through on the "deal," choose a second person and repeat the "game show" with the second kind of candy.)

This is exactly like the "deal" God wants to make with us. The first candy given back represents 10 percent. It is called the tithe. In Malachi 3:10, God says that we can prove Him with this deal. He provides us with the things we need, and He blesses us in what we do. Our part of God's "deal" is to give Him the tithe. One out of 10.

Do you think that's a good deal?

God always keeps His part of any deal. This is the only place in God's Word that tells us He will prove it! Let God prove to you how good and faithful He is. The tithe belongs to Him, and the rest is ours. Now, that's a true sign that He loves and blesses us big-time!

Series: Sweet Life

Home Bible Study for Kids • Week 11: FAITH

DAY 4: ACADEMY LAB — THE HOPE MAGNET

 **Suggested Time:** 10 minutes

 **Memory Verse:** Faith is the confidence that what we hope for will actually happen; it gives us assurance about things we cannot see. —Hebrews 11:1

Supplies: ☐ 1 Large, strong magnet, ☐ A variety of objects that can be drawn to the magnet (ex: paper clips, nails, tacks, fingernail clippers, etc.)

Lesson Instructions:

Today, I have something everyone likes to play with—a magnet. I also have a lot of objects to test.

Let's see which things are drawn to the magnet and which things aren't. *(Take a few minutes to experiment with the magnet. You may want to let the kids collect things from around the house to test.)*

This has been a fun experiment, which brings me to my point. I actually want to talk to you about another kind of magnet, a spiritual magnet, called *faith*. In Hebrews 11:1 it says, "Faith is the confidence that what we hope for will actually happen; it gives us assurance about things we cannot see."

Some of you may not completely understand what that verse is saying, so let me explain it this way: Let's say this paper clip is something you're hoping for.

Maybe you're hoping that your dad gets a better job so he doesn't have to work at night; then he could be home in the evenings, and your family could spend more time together. So, this paper clip is a new job for dad. This magnet is your faith. You believe God's Word that says when you put the Lord first, all other things in your life will be taken care of. That is trusting in God, and it makes the faith magnet strong. Let's see how this hope paper clip reacts to the faith magnet. *(Demonstrate the paper clip being drawn to the magnet.)*

Kids, when your faith magnet is strong, it will draw the things you're hoping for every time, when they are in line with God's purposes!

Notes: _____
_____
_____
_____
_____
_____
_____

Series: Sweet Life

Home Bible Study for Kids • Week 11: FAITH

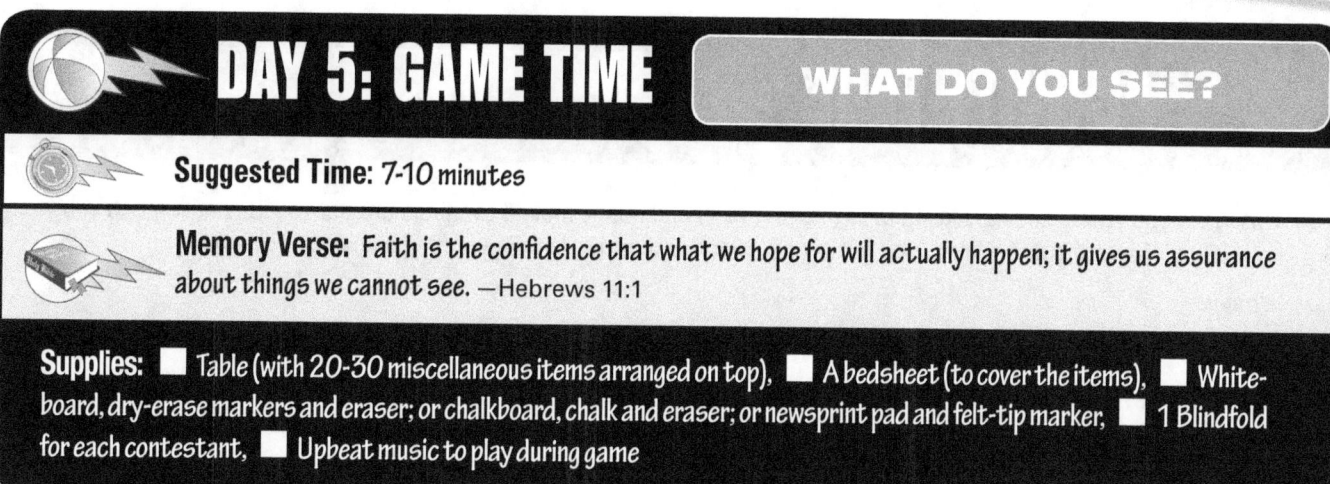

DAY 5: GAME TIME — WHAT DO YOU SEE?

Suggested Time: 7-10 minutes

Memory Verse: Faith is the confidence that what we hope for will actually happen; it gives us assurance about things we cannot see. —Hebrews 11:1

Supplies: ☐ Table (with 20-30 miscellaneous items arranged on top), ☐ A bedsheet (to cover the items), ☐ Whiteboard, dry-erase markers and eraser; or chalkboard, chalk and eraser; or newsprint pad and felt-tip marker, ☐ 1 Blindfold for each contestant, ☐ Upbeat music to play during game

Prior to Game:

This game can be played with 2 teams or as an individual contest.

Place a whiteboard, chalkboard or newsprint pad in front of the room, so everyone can see it.

Cover the miscellaneous items on the table with a sheet before they can be viewed.

Place blindfolds on the contestants.

Have contestants who are waiting to play leave the room, so they can't see or hear the answers of previous players.

Game Instructions:

Lead the first blindfolded contestant to the table.

Remove the bedsheet and allow each contestant to feel the objects for about 45 seconds.

Re-cover the objects on the table, remove the blindfold and allow the child to write on the whiteboard, chalkboard or newsprint sheet each item they can remember.

Allow 1 minute for each contestant to write down the items he/she remembers, reminding the audience not to shout out the answers. Record how many correct answers each player writes down. Erase the board or tear off the newsprint sheet for the next contestant.

Game Goal:

The one who remembers and writes the most objects accurately, wins.

Final Word:

We can "see" things without using our eyes. While the kids were touching objects on the table, they were "seeing" the objects in their minds. This reminds us that we can "see" things in our hearts, before we actually see them with our eyes—just like Hebrews 11:1 tells us! *(Have the kids recite that verse with you.)*

Series: Sweet Life

Home Bible Study for Kids • Week 11: FAITH

ACTIVITY PAGE — WHAT IS IT? COLOR-BY-SHAPE

This week you've learned how to stand strong for Jesus and not be moved by things around you. See how much you've learned by answering this riddle. Color the spaces below according to the guide to discover the answer.

What is:

- A gift from heaven?
- Something everyone receives?
- Something that gives you confidence that your prayers will be answered?
- Not based on what you see, hear, taste or touch?

WHAT IS IT?
COLOR-BY-SHAPE

Color guide:
- 8-point star: BLUE
- Octagon: GREEN
- Circle: RED
- Diamond: BLUE
- Triangle: GREEN
- Heart: BLUE
- Square: RED

Series: Sweet Life

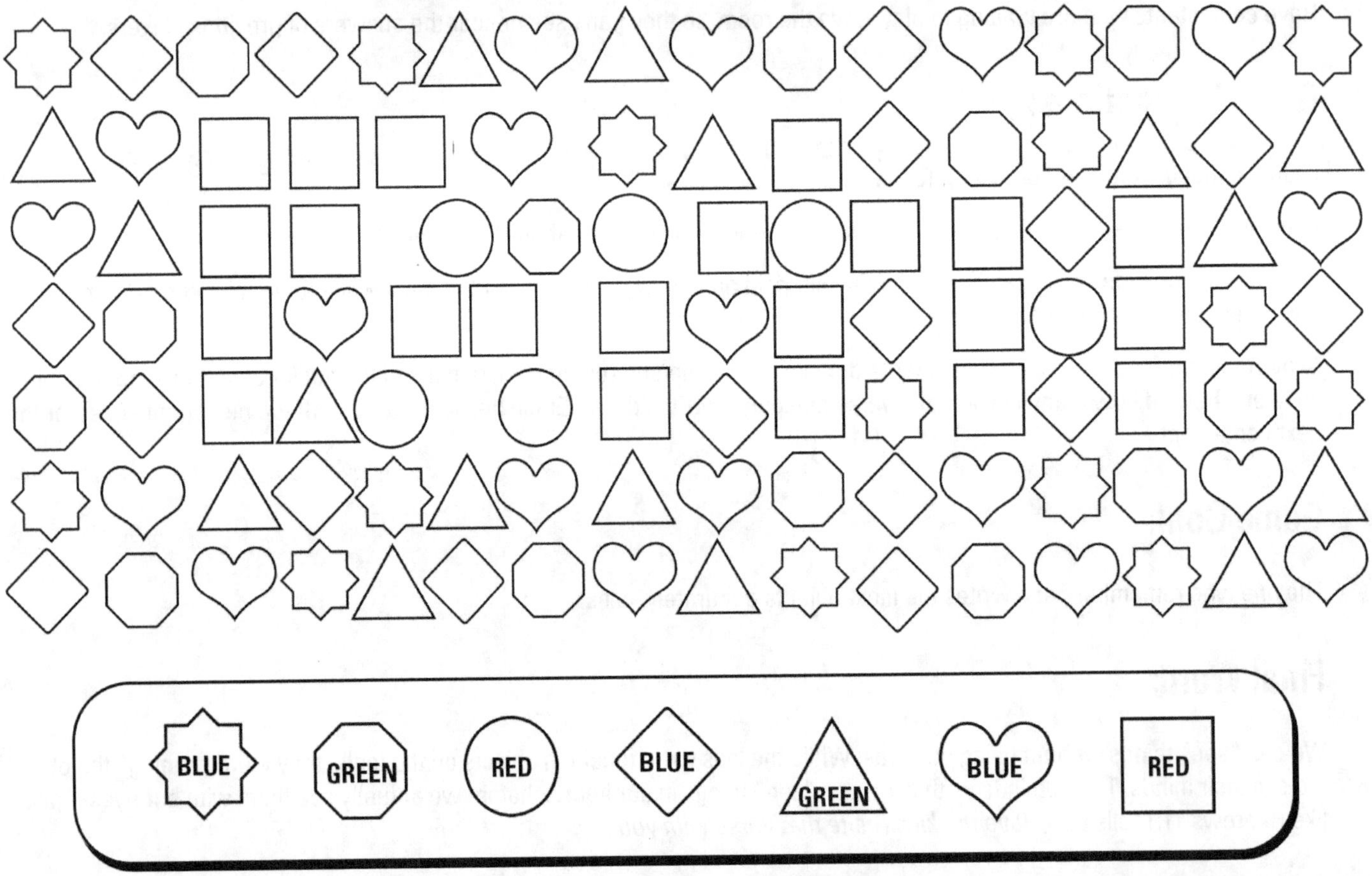

WEEK 12: HOPE

 **DAY 1:** BIBLE LESSON—JOSHUA PREPARES TO CONQUER ▸ PG 168

 **DAY 2:** REAL DEAL—ABRAHAM LINCOLN ▸ PG 170

 **DAY 3:** GIVING LESSON—BRING YOUR OFFERING ▸ PG 173

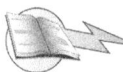 **DAY 4:** OBJECT LESSON—WHAT'S INSIDE? ▸ PG 174

 **DAY 5:** GAME TIME—FLYING DISK FLING ▸ PG 175

 **BONUS:** ACTIVITY PAGE—PROMISED LAND CROSSWORD PUZZLE ▸ PG 177

 **Memory Verse:** And hope does not disappoint us, because God has poured out his love into our hearts by the Holy Spirit, whom he has given us.
—Romans 5:5 NIV-84

Home Bible Study for Kids • Week 12: HOPE

WEEK 12: SNAPSHOT — HOPE

DAY	TYPE OF LESSON	LESSON TITLE	SUPPLIES
Day 1	Bible Lesson	Joshua Prepares to Conquer	None
Day 2	Real Deal	Abraham Lincoln	**Optional costume/props:** White button-up shirt and bow tie, Top hat, Dark suit, Beard, $1 and $5 Bill, 1 Penny
Day 3	Giving Lesson	Bring Your Offering	A $5 bill, Offering container
Day 4	Object Lesson	What's Inside?	1 Pastry turnover, 1 Corn dog (dough-covered frankfurter), 1 Cream-filled cupcake
Day 5	Game Time	Flying Disk Fling	20-25 Empty plastic soda bottles, 20-25 Prizes (small prizes, candy, etc., to fit inside the soda bottles), 1 Plastic flying disk, $1 or $5 or $10 Bill, Upbeat music
Bonus	Activity Page	Promised Land Crossword Puzzle	1 Copy for each child

Lesson Introduction:

Try to get children to really think about what they are hearing during these devotional times. During this lesson, I usually ask a number of children to name something they are hoping for. Steer them toward hopes that line up with the Word of God. Those hopes are powerful!

If we are to expect the force of hope to work in our lives, we must identify what hopes we have in our hearts. After that, it is a matter of asking God according to the Scriptures, aiming our faith and speaking words that can begin to bring our hopes into manifestation. This is a great opportunity for the kids to see how faith, hope and our words work together. With this combination, God always wins!

Commander Dana
—Commander Dana

Series: Sweet Life

Home Bible Study for Kids • Week 12: HOPE

Lesson Outline:

This week, as you train your children in the things of God, help them understand that God has given them desires and talents, and He's given them ideas for how to put their desires and talents together for His glory. Encourage your children to trust God to accomplish His plan for their lives in due season. God is faithful, and what He begins, He will accomplish!

I. WE WERE CREATED TO HAVE HOPE

    a. God created each of us with hope inside.

    b. In fact, our Father had big hopes when He created *us!*

    c. God wants us to have the desires of our hearts. Psalm 37:4

II. JOSHUA HAD A REALLY BIG HOPE

    a. God had promised a special land for Israel. Genesis 13:14-15

    b. Because of the doubters all around him, Joshua had to hold on to his hope for 40 years. He walked around in the desert with hopeless doubters for all those years, but he never let go of his own hope.

    c. When your faith takes aim at your hope, it keeps working until the job is done!

III. NEVER GIVE UP

    a. Hope that is turned aside is bad for the spirit. Proverbs 13:12

    b. Don't ever, ever, ever let go of a godly hope! Be like Joshua, who kept hoping for what God promised even when the people around him had given up.

    c. When dreams come true, it brings life and strength.

Remember, kids who hope until their hope happens are strong! Think big and hope big, just like Joshua, a true "hope hero"!

Notes: _____

_____

_____

_____

_____

Series: Sweet Life

Home Bible Study for Kids • Week 12: HOPE

DAY 1: BIBLE LESSON — JOSHUA PREPARES TO CONQUER

Memory Verse: And hope does not disappoint us, because God has poured out his love into our hearts by the Holy Spirit, whom he has given us. —Romans 5:5 NIV-84

After the Israelites had wandered in the desert for 40 years, Moses died, and God raised up a new leader in young Joshua. Forty years is a long time to wait expectantly for something that God has promised! In fact, as you read the passage with your family today, you will notice that God repeatedly encourages Joshua to be strong and courageous. In other words, God was telling Joshua to have hope that He, the Lord Jehovah, would be with Joshua as he engaged in the extremely difficult task of leading a challenging people to the land of promise. Joshua was successful, which is exactly what the Lord promised him! God always keeps His Word. We can count on it!

Read Joshua 1:1-11:

After the death of Moses the Lord's servant, the Lord spoke to Joshua son of Nun, Moses' assistant. He said, "Moses my servant is dead. Therefore, the time has come for you to lead these people, the Israelites, across the Jordan River into the land I am giving them. I promise you what I promised Moses: 'Wherever you set foot, you will be on land I have given you—from the Negev wilderness in the south to the Lebanon mountains in the north, from the Euphrates River in the east to the Mediterranean Sea in the west, including all the land of the Hittites.' No one will be able to stand against you as long as you live. For I will be with you as I was with Moses. I will not fail you or abandon you.

"Be strong and courageous, for you are the one who will lead these people to possess all the land I swore to their ancestors I would give them. Be strong and very courageous. Be careful to obey all the instructions Moses gave you. Do not deviate from them, turning either to the right or to the left. Then you will be successful in everything you do. Study this Book of Instruction continually. Meditate on it day and night so you will be sure to obey everything written in it. Only then will you prosper and succeed in all you do. This is my command—be strong and courageous! Do not be afraid or discouraged. For the Lord your God is with you wherever you go."

Joshua then commanded the officers of Israel, "Go through the camp and tell the people to get their provisions ready. In three days you will cross the Jordan River and take possession of the land the Lord your God is giving you."

Discussion Questions:

1. **What happens at the beginning of this passage?**
   Moses died and God appointed Joshua as the new leader of Israel.

2. **What was Joshua's job?**
   He had to lead the children of Israel to the land God promised them.

3. **What did God say to Joshua three times?**
   God told him to be strong and courageous!

4. **Why do you think God repeated Himself? Wasn't once enough?**
   He probably repeated this to make sure that Joshua understood that he needed to trust in God rather than man.

5. What did Joshua do when God finished talking to him?
He immediately went out to obey God and tell the people what they should do.

6. What does this tell us about Joshua?
He had faith and hope in God. He trusted that God would fulfill His Word.

7. Are there any areas in your life you feel are difficult to trust and hope in God and His Word?
Allow for responses.

Notes: _____
_____
_____
_____
_____
_____
_____
_____
_____
_____
_____
_____
_____
_____
_____
_____
_____
_____
_____
_____

Home Bible Study for Kids • Week 12: HOPE

DAY 2: REAL DEAL — ABRAHAM LINCOLN

Memory Verse: And hope does not disappoint us, because God has poured out his love into our hearts by the Holy Spirit, whom he has given us.—Romans 5:5 NIV-84

Concept: Highlighting an interesting historical place, figure or event that illustrates the theme of the day. The theme of the day is hope.

Media: If you have the technical capability, show media photos of Abraham Lincoln available on various websites. If you do not have this capability, you may print out photos from the Internet to show the kids or check out a book or documentary about Abraham Lincoln from the library.

Teacher Tip: Entering in costume is an attention grabber for the kids. Be familiar with the material and have pictures available to show.

Optional Costume/Props: ☐ White, button-up shirt and bow tie, ☐ Top hat, ☐ Dark suit, ☐ Hair neatly combed, ☐ Beard, ☐ $1 and $5 Bill, ☐ 1 Penny

Intro:

Today, we're talking about hope—a hope that never gives up. Jesus had hope so strong, He didn't give up when things looked impossible.

What was His hope? Jesus' hope was to rescue the world from sin and death.

There's another man we will learn about today who had hope and never gave up.

Does this $5 bill give anyone a clue?

This person had a hope to do something that looked impossible.

What was his hope?

His hope was to put an end to slavery in America. So, at the age of 23, Abraham Lincoln set out to make his mark as a leader in our nation.

Lesson Instructions:
Abraham's High Hopes:

Abraham Lincoln was born in a log cabin in 1809, to a poor farmer, and only went to school for a year and a half. But, after the death of his mother when Abraham was only 9 years old, his father married Sarah Bush Johnson who strongly encouraged him to read and write. As Abraham grew, he became an avid reader. His humble beginnings did not prevent hope from growing its seed in his heart.

During this time in history, many Americans owned slaves, but when Abraham grew up, he tried to convince leaders that slavery was wrong. Not everyone agreed. The arguments about slavery helped Abraham realize something—if he wanted to make a BIG impact, he needed to have a BIG voice. He became a lawyer, and in 1834 was elected to the Illinois state legislature. From 1847-1849, he served in the U.S. House of Representatives.

What position would allow Abraham Lincoln to have the biggest voice and most powerful impact?

Only the most influential voice—president of the United States—would be enough to have his voice heard throughout his world. This could have been a difficult goal, but Abraham Lincoln wasn't a quitter. It took almost 30 years for him to attain his goal and become president!

Rough Road:

Winning the presidency was a huge mark of success, but Abraham's road to ending slavery had only begun. He had no idea the road would be so rough. In 1861, President Lincoln began using his big voice to bring change, and that angered many people! Slavery was the foundation of the South's economy and deeply embedded in much of the culture. While individual Southerners did not like the idea of slavery, they were also afraid of "big government" and the potential for the northern states to begin to control their economy and essentially their land. As with any national attitudes, the causes are multiple and complex, but the South essentially began fighting for what they considered their rights, initiating the bloody war known as the War Between the States or the Civil War, one of the most brutal, bloodiest wars in U.S. history. It divided the nation as Americans in the northern regions fought against Americans in the southern region of the country.

One of the most notorious battles of the Civil War was fought at Gettysburg. It was so terrible, that President Lincoln lost one-third of the northern army and had to recruit many more soldiers to fight. Even people in the North started doubting President Lincoln's choices, wondering if the determining issue was truly slavery or something less heroic. The people in New York were so upset, they began destroying the city in an effort to force President Lincoln's attention to their anger and frustration over the long and brutal war. Many Americans were afraid that the war against slavery would destroy the nation forever, and they pressured Lincoln to stop this continual fighting.

But, no one was more determined than Abraham Lincoln. He knew slavery was wrong, and he would do whatever it took to free the slaves. Abraham Lincoln didn't like how slaves were being treated by their owners and felt that it was wrong for one human to own another. He believed all men were created equal and should have the same freedom to live and enjoy life. Abraham Lincoln kept his hope alive, ultimately freeing more than 3 million slaves with the "Emancipation Proclamation."

Victory:

Four hard years and many battles later, the Civil War finally ended. At the end of the war, Abraham Lincoln was re-elected as president. The long road to healing and restoration of the nation and giving former slaves the freedom they deserved, had begun. One of the first things Lincoln completed in his second term in office was the drafting of the 13th Amendment to the United States Constitution. Basically, this amendment was a new law for the nation that would do away with slavery forever! There was just one final step to making this dream come true—a vote by the country's leaders. The first time this amendment was proposed, it failed so, once again, President Lincoln went to work, talking with leaders about the significance of this amendment. The second time around, the amendment passed. Abraham's dream had finally come true!

Making History:

Abraham Lincoln contributed in other ways during his time as president of the United States. He declared "Thanksgiving" an official national holiday. Did you know that until President Lincoln's declaration, "Thanksgiving" had only been a holiday that was celebrated once in a great while? By the time he was president, it hadn't been celebrated in 50 years! Abraham Lincoln knew that Americans had much to be thankful for and should celebrate this holiday at the same time

Home Bible Study for Kids • Week 12: HOPE

every year. Thanksgiving dinner can surely make us all thankful. Way to go, Abraham Lincoln!

Outro:

Next time you face something that seems impossible, pull out a penny and remember President Lincoln. He had hope that never quit, and thanks to him, America changed forever! Who knows, maybe your hope will change the world…and because Abraham Lincoln inspires us to never, ever give up, he is today's Real Deal.

Notes: _____
_____
_____
_____
_____
_____
_____
_____
_____
_____
_____
_____
_____
_____
_____
_____

Series: Sweet Life

Home Bible Study for Kids • Week 12: HOPE

DAY 3: GIVING LESSON — BRING YOUR OFFERING

Suggested Time: 10 minutes

Offering Scripture: But the king replied to Araunah, "No, I insist on buying it, for I will not present burnt offerings to the Lord my God that have cost me nothing." So David paid him fifty pieces of silver for the threshing floor and the oxen. —2 Samuel 24:24

Teacher Tip: Before you begin, ask one of the kids to help you with this lesson. Give him or her a $5 bill to hold until you call on them. When you ask for his/her help, he/she will come up and "give" you the offering.

Supplies: ☐ A $5 bill, ☐ Offering container

Lesson Instructions:

(Holding the offering container in your hand, invite your helper to join you.)

Who can guess what (name the child) just did?

(The correct answer would be "gave an offering.")

That's right, kids. At least it looks like an offering! But I want to tell you a story from God's Word that tells us something important about offerings like this one. It's found in 2 Samuel 24. King David needed a place to build an altar to offer a sacrifice to God. But then, something interesting happened. A man named Araunah had a place that would work perfectly for the king to build his altar and make his offering to God. Araunah told the king he could have his threshing floor for free. Not only that, Araunah said the king could even have oxen and wood for the offering as well. What a good deal! But, wait a minute! Listen to what King David told Araunah: "'No, I insist on buying it, for I will not present burnt offerings to the Lord that have cost me nothing,' so David paid him fifty pieces of silver for the threshing floor and the oxen" (2 Samuel 24:24).

It's wonderful when your mom or dad gives you money to put in the offering. That's one of the ways our parents help us learn to give to God. But what King David shows us here is that sometimes we need to give our own offerings to God. Let me challenge you to think about that when you get your offering ready to bring to church this week. I can promise you one thing: When you do…God will bless you big-time!

Notes: _____
_____
_____
_____
_____

Series: Sweet Life

Home Bible Study for Kids • Week 12: HOPE

DAY 4: OBJECT LESSON — WHAT'S INSIDE?

Suggested Time: 10 minutes

Key Scripture: Delight yourself also in the Lord, and He will give you the desires and secret petitions of your heart. —Psalm 37:4 AMP

Supplies: ☐ 1 Pastry turnover, ☐ 1 Corn dog (dough-covered frankfurter), ☐ 1 Cream-filled cupcake

Lesson Instructions:

(Instead of actually preparing a recipe, we're going to check out some foods that are already prepared. You don't have to do anything—there's no cutting, boiling, mashing or stirring required. These are ready to go!)

Can you tell me what all three of these foods have in common?

(Allow time for input from the kids.)

That's right! They all have a filling, something extra on the inside. This is called a *turnover*.

Raise your hand if you really like turnovers. What do they have on the inside?

There are different kinds, but let's check and see what's inside this one. *(Break open the turnover and show the filling. Let kids smell it up close.)*

This next item is one of my favorite things to eat at the fair (carnival).

What is it?

It's a corn dog (dough-covered, deep-fried frankfurter).

Tell me what's on the inside.

Yes, a hot dog (frankfurter)! This is making me hungry for lunch! And, now for the last, delicious item…

Who knows what this is?

A cupcake? Yes, but not just any cupcake!

What's the surprise on the inside for the person who bites into this?

Ooooo, it's a creamy filling! All these foods have something inside them that was placed there by the people who made them.

Did you know that you have a Maker, God, who put something special inside *you*?

Just like the baker put a cream filling inside this cupcake, our heavenly Father filled us with hope. Psalm 37:4 says, "Delight yourself also in the Lord, and He will give you the desires and secret petitions of your heart" (AMP).

God put special hopes and dreams inside each of us. Corn dogs and cupcakes may have something yummy on the inside, but it's nothing compared to the "hope filling" God put inside us!

Series: Sweet Life

Home Bible Study for Kids • Week 12: HOPE

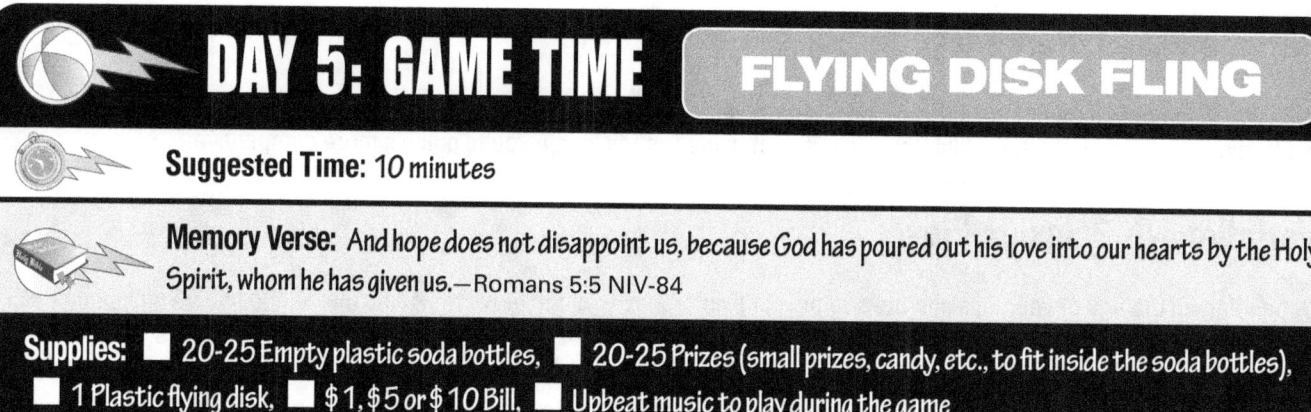

DAY 5: GAME TIME — FLYING DISK FLING

Suggested Time: 10 minutes

Memory Verse: And hope does not disappoint us, because God has poured out his love into our hearts by the Holy Spirit, whom he has given us.—Romans 5:5 NIV-84

Supplies:
- ☐ 20-25 Empty plastic soda bottles
- ☐ 20-25 Prizes (small prizes, candy, etc., to fit inside the soda bottles)
- ☐ 1 Plastic flying disk
- ☐ $1, $5 or $10 Bill
- ☐ Upbeat music to play during the game

Prior to Game:

Place 1 small prize inside each empty soda bottle.

On the inside of 1 bottle lid, color a red star. This bottle will be the "Bonus Bottle."

Place the prize-filled soda bottles in various locations around 1 area of your yard or porch, away from windows.

Game Instructions:

Teach the memory verse.

To play the game, 1 player will say the memory verse. Once the designated player has repeated the verse, he/she has earned 1 opportunity to throw the flying disk.

If a player knocks over the "Bonus Bottle" containing the red star in the lid, he/she will win the $1, $5 or $10 bill!

If a player is unable to knock over a bottle with the flying disk, that player will be out of the game. (Consider giving a small candy for successfully saying the memory verse.)

If a player is able to knock over a prize-filled bottle, that player receives the prize located inside the bottle and the game moves on to the next player. (Remove the empty bottle from the play area.)

If several bottles are knocked over with 1 throw of the flying disk, that player will receive a prize from the first bottle hit.

The knocked-over bottles are then put back in place and the next player takes a turn.

Game Goal:

The goal of this game is to fling the flying disk and knock over a soda bottle.

Final Word:

Never give up. No matter how many times you miss your goal, never let go of your godly hope!

Series: Sweet Life

Variation No. 1: Park Play

Take the soda bottle game to the park and take regular-sized flying disks. Spread out across the area, each person choosing a different colored disk for the "ultimate" competition! Invite friends to join you to make it more competitive.

Variation No. 2: Inside Play

Depending on the age of your kids and the size of your living room, you can move the game inside and use a soft, sponge ball as a bowling ball and the bottles for bowling pins. The player who mows down the most pins in a given round gets to choose a prize and eliminate that bottle from the lineup for the next player.

Variation No. 3: Flying Disk Golf

If your kids are a little older, take the game to a park and play a round of flying disk golf. If players score well in a round, deliver the prize. In this variation, there is no need for the soda bottles or the prizes inside. Use ice cream cones for the prizes or other goodies you know will motivate your kids to learn the memory verse and have fun.

Notes: _____
_____
_____
_____
_____
_____
_____
_____
_____
_____
_____
_____
_____
_____
_____
_____

Home Bible Study for Kids • Week 12: HOPE

ACTIVITY PAGE — PROMISED LAND CROSSWORD PUZZLE

Memory Verse: And hope does not disappoint us, because God has poured out his love into our hearts by the Holy Spirit, whom he has given us. —Romans 5:5 NIV-84

This week you studied how Joshua had hope that God would fulfill His promise and give the Israelites the Promised Land. It wasn't easy, but Joshua continued listening to the Lord and remained strong and courageous. He didn't give up. Now, it's your turn to not give up. Using words from this week's Bible Lesson, complete this crossword puzzle.

PROMISED LAND CROSSWORD PUZZLE

Across
3. The river the Israelites crossed
4. Led the Israelites out of Egypt
6. Family members who lived ages ago
7. Moses' assistant
8. To order or instruct
9. The river in the East
10. Person who provides service to others
12. A region in its natural state where there are trees and wild animals, but no people living there

Down
1. Brave
2. A statement of how to do something
5. Mighty
11. The opposite of life

Series: Sweet Life

Home Bible Study for Kids • Week 12: HOPE

ANSWER KEY

			¹C									²I	
	³J	O	R	D	A	N						N	
	U							⁴M	O	S	E	S	
	R				⁵B							T	
	⁶A	N	C	E	S	T	O	R	S			R	
	G				A			⁷J	O	S	H	U	A
	E				V							C	
	⁸C	O	M	M	A	N	D	⁹E	U	P	H	R	A	T	E	S
	U											I	
	¹⁰S	E	R	V	A	N	T					O	
							¹¹D					N	
				¹²W	I	L	D	E	R	N	E	S	S
							A						
							T						
							H						

Notes: _____

_____

_____

_____

_____

_____

_____

_____

_____

_____

_____

_____

Series: Sweet Life

WEEK 13: LOVE

 DAY 1: BIBLE LESSON—THE VINE AND THE BRANCHES ▶ PG 182

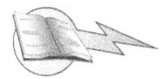 DAY 2: READ-ALOUD—THE LOVE PACKAGE ▶ PG 184

 DAY 3: GIVING LESSON—AN ENDLESS SUPPLY ▶ PG 186

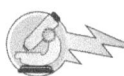 DAY 4: ACADEMY LAB—WHAT DO YOU SEE? ▶ PG 187

 DAY 5: GAME TIME—LOVE HOP ▶ PG 188

 BONUS: ACTIVITY PAGE—HIDDEN HEARTS ▶ PG 189

 **Memory Verse:** *God is love, and all who live in love live in God, and God lives in them.*
1 John 4:16b

Home Bible Study for Kids • Week 13: LOVE

WEEK 13: SNAPSHOT — LOVE

DAY	TYPE OF LESSON	LESSON TITLE	SUPPLIES
Day 1	Bible Lesson	The Vine and the Branches	None
Day 2	Read-Aloud	The Love Package	None
Day 3	Giving Lesson	An Endless Supply	A small clear container with a lid, A bag of candy
Day 4	Academy Lab	What Do You See?	A lab coat (for the teacher), A pointer, An eye chart
Day 5	Game Time	Love Hop	2 Top hats, 2 Buckets, Lots of small hearts cut from card stock, Masking tape, Upbeat music
Bonus	Activity Page	Hidden Hearts	1 Copy for each child

Lesson Introduction:

One of the most rewarding things I experienced in Superkid Academy happened when we challenged the kids to love one another the way Jesus commanded. We suggested a few simple ways they could be thoughtful, friendly and servant-minded. The results were amazing! Within a couple of weeks we had boys and girls giving to others, offering their highly prized front-row seats, and nearly overwhelming first-time guests with hospitality! I realized right then that children want to do what they hear preached. It is our job to find ways to let them "try it out"! Be creative with your kids, and get ready to see an atmosphere of love grow in your home that will resound through the entire family!

Commander Dana
—Commander Dana

Series: Sweet Life

Home Bible Study for Kids • Week 13: LOVE

Lesson Outline:

God created every person with the desire to be loved. It's a need hard-wired into us, but as God's children, we aren't only called to be loved, we are called to love others. Our heavenly Father desires us to share the love, compassion and kindness we have received from Him, with others—believers as well as unbelievers. As you teach this lesson, emphasize that love should be the basis of our motivations. It should be what drives us to share Jesus with the lost, give to those in need and even succeed in our godly calling. God wants to share His love with the world, and we are the means through which He does it. What a glorious calling!

I. EVERY PERSON NEEDS LOVE

   a. Every person on earth needs love in his or her life.

   b. Jesus told us that love and God are the same! 1 John 4:16

   c. The secret to finding true love is to find God.

II. LOVE IS THE BIGGEST COMMANDMENT Matthew 22:37-38

   a. When we care about others, it is like caring for Jesus. Matthew 25:40

   b. God's kind of love is unselfish; it thinks of others first. If you want to know whether God's love is working through you, ask this question: "Am I caring about others like God wants me to?"

   c. When you care about people, it shows them that God does too!

III. JESUS IS THE VINE, WE ARE THE BRANCHES John 15:5

   a. Branches receive their life from the vine. You never see a tree branch disconnected from a tree that looks very good!

   b. Branches that disconnect from the vine become dead and dry. That's how we get on the inside if we do not stay closely connected to Jesus. He is our "Love Connection."

   c. The closer you stay to Jesus, the healthier your love is. It can't help but grow!

Notes: _____

_____

_____

_____

Series: Sweet Life

Home Bible Study for Kids • Week 13: LOVE

DAY 1: BIBLE LESSON — THE VINE AND THE BRANCHES

Memory Verse: *God is love, and all who live in love live in God, and God lives in them.* —1 John 4:16b

This week's lesson on love is a tremendous opportunity to focus on character and relationships, first with God and then with each other. If each family member allows God to do His work within them, it prepares the way for God to have His way within the whole family and ultimately, the community. The love your family shares will attract others to the gospel. They'll see the difference. Get ready to be busier than ever, just loving people!

Read John 15:1-17:

I am the true grapevine, and my Father is the gardener. He cuts off every branch of mine that doesn't produce fruit, and he prunes the branches that do bear fruit so they will produce even more. You have already been pruned and purified by the message I have given you. Remain in me, and I will remain in you. For a branch cannot produce fruit if it is severed from the vine, and you cannot be fruitful unless you remain in me.

Yes, I am the vine; you are the branches. Those who remain in me, and I in them, will produce much fruit. For apart from me you can do nothing. Anyone who does not remain in me is thrown away like a useless branch and withers. Such branches are gathered into a pile to be burned. But if you remain in me and my words remain in you, you may ask for anything you want, and it will be granted! When you produce much fruit, you are my true disciples. This brings great glory to my Father.

I have loved you even as the Father has loved me. Remain in my love. When you obey my commandments, you remain in my love, just as I obey my Father's commandments and remain in his love. I have told you these things so that you will be filled with my joy. Yes, your joy will overflow!

This is my commandment: Love each other in the same way I have loved you. There is no greater love than to lay down one's life for one's friends. You are my friends if you do what I command. I no longer call you slaves, because a master doesn't confide in his slaves. Now you are my friends, since I have told you everything the Father told me. You didn't choose me. I chose you. I appointed you to go and produce lasting fruit, so that the Father will give you whatever you ask for, using my name. This is my command: Love each other.

Discussion Questions:

1. **How does Jesus describe Himself?**
   Jesus says He is the true vine.

2. **How does Jesus describe God?**
   Jesus says that God is the true Gardener.

3. **What does God do with branches that don't bear fruit?**
   He cuts them off.

4. **So what is our job as branches?**
   Our job is to bear fruit.

Series: Sweet Life

5. **How do we bear fruit?**
   We must remain in Jesus to bear fruit; apart from Him, we can't do anything.

6. **What is the purpose of bearing fruit?**
   The purpose of bearing fruit is to bring the Father God glory.

7. **How do we remain in God's love?**
   We obey His commands.

8. **What are His commands?**
   He commands us to love each other as He has loved us.

9. **What do you think God meant when He commanded us to love each other as He loves us?**
   Answers will vary.

10. **Name some ways you can start showing your love to others, especially in our family.**
    Answers will vary, but encourage kids to be practical and specific.

Notes: _____
_____
_____
_____
_____
_____
_____
_____
_____
_____
_____
_____
_____
_____
_____
_____
_____
_____
_____

Home Bible Study for Kids • Week 13: LOVE

DAY 2: READ-ALOUD — THE LOVE PACKAGE

Suggested Time: 15 minutes

Memory Verse: *God is love, and all who live in love live in God, and God lives in them.* —1 John 4:16b

Story:

Claire turned on the radio while working on her nails. As she did, the booming voice of the radio announcer began, "Do you ever feel unloved? Are you tired of feeling like no one loves you for who you are? Have you ever sat around doing your nails just wishing you had someone to talk to?"

Claire looked around, "OK, that's weird."

The announcer continued. "Well, listen up, this offer is for YOU! The 'Love' package can be delivered straight to your home, free of charge. That's right, absolutely free! We are so convinced you'll *love* your new 'Love' package and want to order more, that we're actually giving it away! That's right, giving it away. What have you got to lose? Don't delay! Call now and receive our bonus 'Loving Others' package. Not only will *you* feel loved, you'll love others too! Never again will you find a better deal. Get your phone, and call now! You'll be so glad you did." Then, trailing off with an increase in the speed of his voice, he added, "1 John 4:16 clause applicable in all situations...."

Claire grabbed her cellphone and quickly dialed the number from the radio commercial, drumming her freshly painted nails on her desk as she waited for someone to pick up. "Hi," she said, "I'm calling about the 'Love' package. Uh-huh. Thank you. Oh, wait! Don't you need my address? No? You know where I live? Wow. That IS weird. OK, bye."

Claire sat, wondering how long it would take for her package to arrive. Her thoughts were quickly halted by a knock on her door. As she peered out through the peephole, she realized it was a deliveryman. *Wow! That was fast! How did they do that?*

Claire quickly opened the door and accepted her packages. As the deliveryman turned to leave, Claire called him back, "Hey, wait a sec! I don't think these are my packages. They have these huge labels with 'God' written on them. That's not what I ordered."

The deliveryman smiled, "Ah, so no one told you?"

"Excuse me? What do you mean?" Claire questioned.

The deliveryman patiently paused. "You must have missed the 1 John 4:16 disclaimer at the end of the commercial. That gets a lot of people."

Claire felt like she'd stepped into a church youth group somewhere. "What in the world are you talking about?"

The deliveryman continued. "The 1 John 4:16 clause says that God IS Love. That means receiving God is the same as receiving love. Soooo, if you got the 'God' package, you got the 'Love' package."

Claire laughed. "Well, I can't wait to see what's in my packages! The advertisement promised me it was exactly what I needed. I certainly hope so."

"I've never had anyone send their package back," the deliveryman said. "So I'm sure it is."

THE END

Home Bible Study for Kids • Week 13: LOVE

DISCUSSION QUESTIONS:

1. **What do you think was in Claire's packages?**
   Allow time for various answers.

2. **What was the "1 John 4:16 disclaimer"?**
   Receiving God is the same as receiving Love, so if you ordered the "Love" package, you were ordering the "God" package.

3. **Why was there a "Loving Others" package offered as a bonus?**
   When you experience God's love, not only will you feel loved, you'll love others too!

4. **Why did Claire say the advertisement promised the "Love" package would be exactly what she needed?**
   Everyone needs to know Jesus as their Savior and experience God's love.

Notes: _____

Series: Sweet Life

Home Bible Study for Kids • Week 13: LOVE

DAY 3: GIVING LESSON — AN ENDLESS SUPPLY

 **Suggested Time:** 10 minutes

 **Offering Scripture:** Be generous. Give to the poor. Get yourselves a bank that can't go bankrupt....
—Luke 12:33 MSG

Supplies: ☐ A small, clear container with a lid, ☐ A bag of candy

Prior to Lesson:

Write the word "BANK" on the side of the small, clear container.

Fill the container with candy.

Set aside some extra candy to refill the container.

Lesson Instructions:

Today, I have something you may have never seen before. It's a special type of piggy bank, and the reason it's special is because instead of money, this bank is full of candy. If you're wondering why my bank is full of candy instead of pennies, I'll tell you: It's because I thought it might be more fun to give away candy instead of pennies! Don't you agree? But, I need your help!

Would you like to help me?

All right, here's the plan: This is now your bank, and it's your job to take some of your "money" (the candy) and share it with a few others. My job is to hold the bank for you. Sound good?

(As your child distributes a few pieces of candy to other family members, replenish the bank while the child's back is turned. Repeat this process several times, even allowing him or her to give several pieces of candy to each family member.)

You're a very generous "banker." Look at all the candy you've given away. *(Have the other kids hold up the candy they received.)*

But let's take a look at the bank. *(Show it to the "banker" and ask:)*

Does your bank look like it is about to run out of candy?

It would make sense that this bank would run out of candy because so much was given away.

Why didn't the candy level go down in the bank?

Because every time candy was taken out, more candy was put in to replace what was taken out.

Did you know that's exactly what God does for us when we are generous givers?

In Luke 12:33, MSG, Jesus tells us to "be generous. Give to the poor. Get yourselves a bank that can't go bankrupt...."

Having a bank that doesn't go bankrupt means that it will never run out. How awesome! When we are generous givers, Jesus promised us that it will be like having a bank that never runs out. Why?

Because every time we give, He's right there replacing what we give away, and adding more. With a bank like that, there's no reason to not have a generous heart!

Series: Sweet Life

Home Bible Study for Kids • Week 13: LOVE

DAY 4: ACADEMY LAB — WHAT DO YOU SEE?

Suggested Time: 10 minutes

Memory Verse: God is love, and all who live in love live in God, and God lives in them. —1 John 4:16b

Teacher Tip: Discuss ways to draw closer to God. Perhaps write them on a piece of paper next to the eye chart. A few suggestions for drawing closer to God:
- Read His Word
- Pray for friends and family
- Worship God with all your heart
- Tell someone about God

Supplies: ☐ A lab coat (for the teacher), ☐ A pointer, ☐ An eye chart

Lesson Instructions:

What is this?

Yes! It's an eye chart.

Is there someone who would like to read this chart for me?

(Choose one of your children to read down the chart as far as they can. Then have him/her move closer so he/she can read the smaller lines. Continue this process until he/she can read even the smallest print.)

The closer you came to the chart, the better you could see to read. This reminds me of God's love! In a unique way, God is like this eye chart. The closer we are to Him, the more of His love we can see.

How much of God's love can *you* see? Can you only see a little bit, like the first line on the eye chart, or can you see the whole page of letters?

If you want to have perfect vision for our heavenly Father's love, you don't need a pair of glasses, all you need to do is get closer to Him!

Notes: _____

Series: Sweet Life

 Home Bible Study for Kids • Week 13: LOVE

DAY 5: GAME TIME — LOVE HOP

Suggested Time: 5-10 minutes

Memory Verse: *God is love, and all who live in love live in God, and God lives in them.* —1 John 4:16b

Supplies: ☐ 2 Top hats (often available at party supply stores or toy stores), ☐ 2 Buckets (containing lots of hearts cut from card stock, small enough to be easily caught in the top hat), ☐ Masking tape to create a large, numbered grid (1-12) taped out on the floor, ☐ Upbeat music to play during the game

Prior to Game:

With the masking tape, mark out a rectangular grid on the floor with a number in each section ranging from 1-12.

Make the grid large enough for 1 child to easily stand inside 1 of the numbered sections.

From card stock, cut out heart shapes small enough to be easily caught in the top hat.

Choose 2 people to form a team.

One player will stand inside the grid holding the top hat, while the other player stands on a designated spot outside the grid.

Game Instructions:

Say: "God's Word tells us that He actually lives in those who love Him. The more like God we are, the more love we'll have in our lives. Today, we're going to see who can catch the most 'hearts of love' in his/her top hat!"

To start the game, the leader will call out a number, and the player in the grid must jump to the square with that number in it.

Once the player is in the correct square, the player standing outside the grid will toss a "heart of love" to the teammate inside the grid. Continue to call out numbers so the player inside the grid has to hop to different grid numbers.

The hearts must be caught while the player is standing on the correct number inside the grid. Hearts caught while standing in the wrong section will not count.

Game Goal:

Catch all the hearts in the top hat, or as many as possible.

Final Word:

Loving like God loves takes a lot of work, but it's really fun! This point can be made to the group during and after this game. It's also a great game to emphasize cooperation and patience with your partner.

Series: Sweet Life

Home Bible Study for Kids • Week 13: LOVE

ACTIVITY PAGE — HIDDEN HEARTS

Memory Verse: *God is love, and all who live in love live in God, and God lives in them.* —1 John 4:16b

This week you learned how important love is to your Christian life—love for God and love for others. Around the world, people are searching for true love, but if you know Jesus, you have experienced true love because God is Love, and He has already shown just how much He loves you through Jesus' sacrifice for you. Now, see how well you can search out 25 hearts in this garden picture.

Series: Sweet Life

Home Bible Study for Kids • Week 13: LOVE

Notes: _____

_____
_____
_____
_____
_____
_____
_____
_____
_____
_____
_____
_____
_____
_____
_____
_____
_____
_____
_____
_____
_____
_____
_____
_____
_____
_____
_____
_____
_____

Series: Sweet Life

ALSO AVAILABLE:

- Praise and Worship CDs with Singalong Tracks
- 24-Song Praise and Worship Video DVD
- Classic Superkid Academy Movies and Novels
- Extra Handouts, Dinnertime Devotionals, Coloring Papers, Games and More.

And, remember, to access your Bonus Downloads Section, please use the following URL:

http://www.superkidacademy.com/downloads

Need more supplies or information?
Just go to:
SUPERKIDACADEMY.COM